Listening

Listening

Its Impact at All Levels
on Reading and the Other Language Arts

Revised Edition

Sara W. Lundsteen
North Texas State University

ERIC Clearinghouse on Reading and Communication Skills
National Institute of Education

National Council of Teachers of English
1111 Kenyon Road, Urbana, Illinois 61801

Book Design: Tom Kovacs

NCTE Stock Number 29498

Published 1979 by the ERIC Clearinghouse on Reading and Communication Skills and the National Council of Teachers of English, 1111 Kenyon Road, Urbana, Illinois 61801

The material in this publication was prepared pursuant to a contract with the National Institute of Education, U.S. Department of Health, Education, and Welfare. Contractors undertaking such projects under government sponsorship are encouraged to express freely their judgment in professional and technical matters. Prior to publication, the manuscript was submitted to the National Council of Teachers of English for critical review and determination of professional competence. This publication has met such standards. Points of view or opinions, however, do not necessarily represent the official view or opinions of either the National Council of Teachers of English or the National Institute of Education.

Library of Congress Cataloging in Publication Data

Lundsteen, Sara W

    Listening, its impact at all levels on reading and other language arts

    Bibliography: p.
    1. Language arts. 2. Reading. 3. Listening.
I. Title.
LB1575.8.L8 1979 372.6 79-14249
ISBN 0-8141-2949-8 (National Council of Teachers of English)

Contents

Foreword

The Educational Resources Information Center (ERIC) is a national information system developed by the U.S. Office of Education and now sponsored by the National Institute of Education (NIE). It provides ready access to descriptions of exemplary programs, research and development efforts, and related information useful in developing more effective educational programs.

Through its network of specialized centers or clearinghouses, each of which is responsible for a particular educational area, ERIC acquires, evaluates, abstracts, and indexes current significant information and lists this information in its reference publications.

ERIC/RCS, the ERIC Clearinghouse on Reading and Communication Skills, disseminates educational information related to research, instruction, and personnel preparation at all levels and in all institutions. The scope of interest of the Clearinghouse includes relevant research reports, literature reviews, curriculum guides and descriptions, conference papers, project or program reviews, and other print materials related to all aspects of reading, English, educational journalism, and speech communication.

The ERIC system has already made available—through the ERIC Document Reproduction Service—much informative data. However, if the findings of specific educational research are to be intelligible to teachers and applicable to teaching, considerable bodies of data must be reevaluated, focused, translated, and molded into an essentially different context. Rather than resting at the point of making research reports readily accessible, NIE has directed the separate clearinghouses to work with professional organizations in developing information analysis papers in specific areas within the scope of the clearinghouses.

ERIC/RCS is pleased to cooperate with the National Council of Teachers of English in making available this revised edition of *Listening*.

Preface

The intention of this book is to build bridges between the study of listening in several disciplines and the needs of the classroom teacher. Listening is important, but we do not appear to know much about it, or how to teach it, or how to integrate it with the other language arts. Little about listening methodology is supported by reliable and replicated research findings. This conclusion is not so much an indictment of experimenters as it is a reflection of the complexities of listening and of children, teachers, classroom instruction, and the environment in which it takes place. It is impossible to encompass, moreover, the breadth of available data on listening. Probably all research, for example, that utilizes speech-using and listening individuals gives some information about listening. Consequently, although references are given to studies and to reviews of research literature, this report represents in large part the predispositions, hunches, points of view, and opinions of one teacher-researcher.

Modern teachers are looking for more than mere "how to do it," cookbook solutions. They know that the challenges facing today's schools are too complex to be solved by simple revision of administrative procedures or by more efficient ways to do what is wrong in a curriculum; therefore, products that promise "instant" results are thrown into the "circular file." Educators are looking for ideas solidly grounded in basic and applied scientific research. While they look for ideas that are practical and feasible, they also look for those that are not simplistic—ideas of intelligent men and women that may be discussed and used by other intelligent men and women. This monograph is dedicated to these people.

The material contained in the 1971 edition of this book has been extensively reworked: all chapters have been rewritten, references have been updated, and new topics and activities have been added. This revision was greatly aided by my work on two other books, *Children Learn to Communicate* and *Ideas into Practice,* both published by Prentice-Hall.

The Introduction, dealing with the priority and value of listening instruction, has two parts: the case is stated for the urgency of more attention to listening, and a plea is made for greater systemization in instruction. Chapters one and two deal with definitions that converge on a model of proficient listening behavior. Chapter three gives a framework for a taxonomy of listening skills. Chapter four describes available measurement, and chapter five evaluates current materials and teaching techniques and lists the instructional roles suggested by the literature. The Appendix provides sample listening lessons for listening centers.

The author wishes to gratefully acknowledge assistance from the Charles F. Kettering Foundation, the University of Texas at Austin, and the University of California, Santa Barbara, which enabled collection and abstraction of studies on listening. The author wishes to express special appreciation to Alvina T. Burrows and to H. Alan Robinson for their helpful critiques and many suggestions for the first edition of this publication. Thanks also to Bernard O'Donnell for his encouragement, suggestions, and many kindnesses concerning this work. Julie M. T. Chan, California State University, Long Beach, furnished annotations of listening materials since 1971 and new lessons for the Appendix. Sue Francis, North Texas State University, also assisted in the literature search.

Introduction

Why put listening first in the language arts? For one reason, listening is the first language skill to appear. Chronologically, children listen before they speak, speak before they read, and read before they write. Moreover, studies of physiological deprivation—specifically, hearing disorders, aphasia, and brain damage—point to a progressive sequence or hierarchical interdependence among these language skills (Brown, 1954). For example, reading may depend so completely upon listening as to appear to be a special extension of listening. What child does not read a selection better after hearing it and talking about it? A filmstrip or movie dealing with *Tom Sawyer* may help a child through Mark Twain's complex prose to the rewards that await. Reading is normally superimposed on a listening foundation: the ability to listen seems to set limits on the ability to read.

The dependence of speaking upon listening is dramatically illustrated by the example of deaf-mutes who are unable to speak because they are unable to hear. Moreover, without reeducation, a person who once heard but who becomes deaf may lose his or her ability to speak within about five years. Writing, in turn is both directly and indirectly dependent upon listening because of its relation to speaking on one hand and to reading on the other. In an early but important study Heider and Heider (1940) found that the compositions of deaf children (eleven to seventeen years) resembled those of hearing children about three years younger. The hearing children used more compound and complex sentences with a larger number of verbs in coordinate and subordinate clauses; the deaf showed practically no increase in clause use with age. The deaf also showed less unity in style, less variety, and rarely wrote of what was a possibility, but rather made simple, flat statements. Quantitative assessment did not reveal the apparent deficit in the thought structures of the deaf (see also Cooper, 1965).

There is nothing new in the statement that listening and speaking have been considered the base for the other language skills and that auditory discrimination has been considered a crucial base for spelling. Teachers in training usually hear that "the development of language skills proceeds from listening to speaking to reading to writing—in that order." But then the teacher is confronted with instructional materials that seem to forget all about listening and speaking. This neglect seems unwise, since listening may be the first step in unlocking progress in any other area related to language—that means science, history, math, the whole of education.

Do the Mass Media Influence Listening?

The importance of listening is based upon several assumptions and speculations: (1) one of our foremost problems today is the influence of mass media, which can produce conformity rather than in-

The Language Mobile

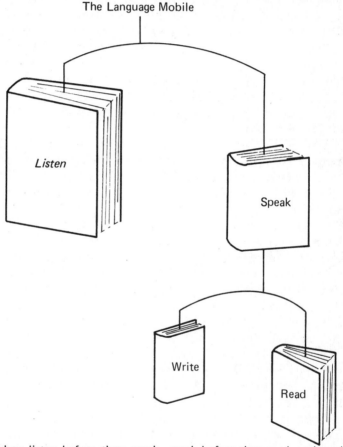

Fig. 1. Children listen before they speak, speak before they read, and read before they write.

dividuality—minds and self-pictures are shaped in the same mold, as if by a giant cookie cutter; (2) people's reactions are influenced by the way they have unconsciously learned to listen; (3) how people have learned to listen strongly affects how they learn to think and to solve problems—they go to "war" in homes, schools, nations, and in the world or they go to "peace" or they just muddle along indecisively, at least partly because of how they have learned to listen.

By the time children end their elementary education, chances are that they have spent more time before the TV set than in school. A significant portion of the children born after 1945 (brought up in their parents' homes, to be sure) have had their imaginative lives, their daydreams, their expectations of the world created by TV.

There is concern about children's capability to communicate—to give and receive signals efficiently. "They simply cannot ask questions!" deplores one first-grade teacher. Since the TV set cannot answer back, children do not develop skill in inquiry. Children may parrot letters of the alphabet learned from a TV program, but they will be unable to put them to intelligent use. Children can have no interaction with a TV set, no experience in influencing behavior and being influenced in return. As one writer put it, having a puppy is, in this sense, far more important to a child than having a TV. From ages 3 to 18 the 22,000 hours spent in passive contemplation of the screen by the average child are stolen from the time needed to learn to relate to brothers, sisters, playmates, parents, grandparents, strangers (see Gall, 1970).

Actually, there are probably no complete villains in the story. All may be simply victims of the unforeseen consequences of a technological revolution. The difficulty may not be solely commercial TV but the fact that we receive its messages almost to the exclusion of other possible messages. The problems thus posed for language development and thought are particularly relevant to teachers of the language arts. What programs are good for children and at what ages? Are such programs as "Sesame Street" the best answer? Only through continued research will we come up with answers to these questions.

Does Noise Pollution Affect Listening?

Noise pollution appears to inhibit our ability to listen. According to a federal report, the overall loudness of noise is doubling every ten years. Moreover, not all sound enters the body through the outer ear; the inner ear is capable of receiving acoustic energy by way of both bone and tissue conduction. Intense sound waves can penetrate the skull, torso, and groin. Sound also produces far more than the sensation of hearing. The sound signal transmitted by the brain goes to almost every nerve center and organ of the body, and sound can influence physical, physiological, emotional, and psychological aspects and responses of the organism.

Researchers at the Educational Facilities Laboratories in New York hypothesize that disruptive noises influence both the effectiveness and the dignity of teaching. Children in the cooperating Dalton School in New York calmed considerably with the change from typical noise-box classrooms to new sound-treated rooms. The deputy health commissioner of Detroit speculated, in a meeting of the American Public Health Association, that part of the tension that erupted in that city's ghetto in the late 1960s may be attributed in part to interrupted sleep. City noise levels far above those required for optimum sleeping can produce insomnia, which in turn breeds instability. Noise can also cause deafness: otologists report that prolonged exposure to a noise level of about 85 decibels (lower than heavy city traffic) can eventually result in loss of hearing for sounds in the range most crucial for understanding human speech. The danger of amplified music (90 to 105 decibels with peaks of 130) has made news. The ears have no lids and are always vulnerable; hearing, like the human heart, might be said to work twenty-four hours a day.

A moderate position contends that sounds or noise may change physiological states. Until it is known that such changes have little or no effect, educators should be aware that noise is a possible health hazard. But perhaps people with limited foresight (similar to those in England who were not convinced of the danger of air pollution until people started dying) would delay until blood runs out of their ears.

The educational implications of a study of noise pollution suggest several areas of attention that need further research and dissemination of results among school people, with the eventual intent to inform children. Educators can accomplish this task in much the same way that curriculum specialists now work with content on ecology and drugs (Brown, 1970). School people should also monitor the noise level of the classroom listening center. If children who are using earphones increase the volume too much while manipulating the controls, they run the risk of irreparable hearing loss through damage to the delicate inner ear. Thus, it is probably inadvisable to allow children to touch the volume controls of earphones. School people also need to be as aware of the listening environment as they have been in the past of room temperature, light, and ventilation.

Is There a Need for Systematic Instruction in Listening?

The last sections stated reasons for stressing listening and set the stage for implying that growth in general and in critical listening skills and understandings in particular is not automatic. If it were, there might be less harm in unconscious assimilations from mass media and other sources. Intelligence and age do not account totally for growth, according to studies designed to promote general and critical listening skills; training helps. (See reviews by Duker, 1969; Olsen, 1966; Russell, 1964; Devine, 1978.) Oakland (1969) inferred that phonemic and nonphonemic auditory discrimination skills may be more closely related to socioeconomic status than to IQ. Children from culturally different and economically disadvantaged homes do not appear to perform as well as their more advantaged peers, as exemplified by the results of the Wepman Auditory Discrimination Test.

Nor does improvement in reading skill automatically result in growth in listening, though there could be some mutual background reinforcement. In fact, listening ability, which may exceed reading comprehension among primary pupils, may become less efficient as reading skill and age increase. Finally, adults may be generally the worst listeners of all (Rossiter, 1970). Lack of systematic training takes its toll. Bad habits practiced for a lifetime are hard to eradicate.

Does Instruction in Listening Improve Reading?

There is some evidence that instruction in listening may bring improvement in reading skills (e.g., Devine, 1967, 1968, 1978; Duker, 1969; Durrell and Murphy, 1953; Schneeberg, 1977). Studies that covered almost all grade and IQ levels indicated that listening instruction may have enhanced reading instruction, especially at the first-grade level. Other studies, however, imply that listening instruction does not improve reading skills (Duker, 1968). Both questions and their answers are highly complex.

If we wait to provide instruction in critical listening, it may be too late. One early research study (Klee, 1949) of children as young as those in the third and fourth grades showed how misconceptions derived from mass media stereotypes of foreigners appeared to be there to stay. For example, in spite of vivid instruction—films, visitations, discussions—Chinese were still thought of as being the evil spy or as doing laundry. Another study (Rosnow, 1972) dealt with prejudicial attitudes in children as young as four years old. If half of all the mental growth a child will ever acquire is possessed, typically, by the age of about four (Carroll, 1968), it seems unprofitable to delay instruction until college.

There may be temptations to forego systematic listening instruction for several reasons, among them the already overcrowded school day and the fact that teachers have never had instruction in listening themselves and therefore do not know how to teach it. False analogies may also provide an excuse: "You have two legs, so you can walk; you have two ears, so you can listen." Perhaps it is too bad that ears do not wiggle when hearing takes place (as eyes move when we read), for maybe the hidden behavior of listening has made us reluctant to accept the challenge of providing the listening instruction needed for improved communication. But possibly a more valid reason for not establishing the systematic instruction according to reading and writing is that listening has been poorly defined. Chapter one attempts to do something about this lack of an adequate definition.

Listening

1 What Is Listening?
Comparisons with
Other Language Arts

If our goal is to work for improvement of the listening process, that process had better be defined as clearly as possible within the current state of knowledge. *Listening,* an ambiguous term, is worth some time and effort to define it. For a quick definition, this will do: "The process by which spoken language is converted to meaning in the mind." Yet, since a final definition of listening is going to affect teaching, there is no more important question to ask than: What is listening?

In this chapter you will find two approaches to a definition of listening: stating attributes and making comparisons with the other language arts—reading, speaking, and writing. In the next chapter a third way of defining the term is attempted: enumerating the operations of a proficient listener. Equipped with these definitions of listening, teachers should be able to so sharpen their perceptions of listening that they become more sensitive educators.

Definition by Attributes

One way to define listening is to list its attributes (ostensive definition). Table 1 presents a partial list of attributes for both listening and reading to show clearly the comparisons that follow. Listening consists of the interaction of all the attributes in the middle column of Table 1.

Comparative Definition

With these attributes in mind, we can now use a broader comparative approach to defining listening. The question is: "What else does listening consist of?" Just as we understand *cold* better by defining *hot,* we understand listening better and interrelate it more skillfully if we compare and contrast it with reading, speaking, and writing.

1

Table 1

Attributes of Listening and Reading

Classification	Listening	Reading
Language		
Minimum features	phonemes	letters
Symbol context	pause	period, semicolon, dash, comma
	stress	italics
	intonation	capitalization
	pitch	paragraphing
	pronunciation	spelling
	timbre	handwriting
	amplitude	type size
Time Pressure	strong, sequential, holding impermanent or requiring equipment for recorded speech	weak, reader can review, see several elements at once; holding limited to the permanence of material used
Human Being		
Personal context	simple to complex	usually absent
Muscular act	none necessary	chiefly eye movement
Malfunction	deafness	blindness
Causes of fatigue	e.g., masking	e.g., illegibility
Feedback	immediate in conversation, review rare	remote, rereading and review possible, usually no immediate opportunity to question author
Emotion	sometimes strong in interaction with other people	usually weak
Physical Science		
Maximum capacity	8,000 bits of information per second	43×10^6 bits of information per second
Vibrations	of air	of light
Field of variation	time	space
Spectrum effects	pitch, timbre	color
Amplitude	loud—soft	bright—dim
Measurement units	decibels	lumens
Science	acoustics	optics

How Does Listening Resemble Reading?

Reading may depend so completely upon listening as to appear to be a special extension of it. Since reading is normally superimposed on a foundation of listening, the ability to listen seems to set limits on the ability to read. A child in need of remedial reading is also a child in need of remedial *listening.* There are many specific links between reading and listening, such as: (1) the act of receiving, (2) analogous features, (3) vocabulary, and (4) common skills of thinking and understanding. Consider them each in turn.

Receiving. Whether a speaker says, "See the bomb," or a writer sends a note to that effect, the receiver in both cases gets material to decode into meaning.

Analogous features. Initially, the process of learning to read may include finding analogies among the components of listening and reading. For example, a beginner may translate and superimpose the symbol read upon the one to which he or she has listened. It seems that no one ever reads totally by vision alone (Edfeldt, 1960; Kavanough and Mattingly, 1972). Most people regress and "sound out" words when they are difficult or unfamiliar *if the words are important to meaning.* Moreover, children need to translate the printed, left-to-right spatial relation of reading into the first-to-last relation of spoken sounds. Once a child has adequate reading skill, the two receptive processes of reading and listening should be mutually supportive. The understanding of a component in one can enhance development in the other. For example, a drop in pitch and a definite pause in oral language can be associated with terminal punctuation in written language.

Vocabulary. There are classroom implications for links between reading and listening vocabularies. "Book language" may be the only medium in which children meet the phrase "If I were" or "I presume." Chances are that they will translate these phrases into their own language when they read them, or will be able to leap over them, or will find them a meaningless stumbling block. In other words, children need to experience language both as a listener and as a speaker before they comprehend it as a reader. As the saying goes, first they need to "get it in the ear." The classroom implications of this relationship are that the size of the *listening* vocabulary may indicate the possibility of improvement in reading; the size of a visual vocabulary may provide one test of reading achievement.

Common skills of thinking and understanding. Listening and reading make use of many of the same feelings, background experiences, concepts, and thought strategies. Processes that go beyond the mere physical acts of seeing and hearing are similar. A book that gives Mary a problem in understanding when she reads it probably gives her the same problem of comprehension when she listens to it.

The physical reception and translation of sounds into meaning through *listening* is different from the reception and translation of print into meaning in *reading*. Learning to efficiently receive a spoken message includes the following:

> Dealing positively with noises that mask[1] or cover up a message
>
> Practicing concentration on and attention to auditory stimuli
>
> Dealing with listener fatigue
>
> Consciously calling up past auditory background (in order to aid in recoding sound to language and in anticipating the spoken message)[2]

Only when listeners are able to perceive accurately what is said are they free to move to the crucial matter of what is meant.

There have been many studies designed to illustrate that teachers can improve listening skills with direct instruction (see Devine, 1978, for a review). There is also some evidence that listening instruction may bring improvement in reading skills in both the early and later grades. For example, Trebilcock (1970) reports one study of improved listening through lessons at the kindergarten level. Duker (1968) reports twelve studies, covering almost all grades and IQ levels, that imply that listening instruction enhanced reading performance. Five studies, however (one with retarded children, one of doubtful design), implied that listening instruction failed to improve reading skills. A project (Witkin, 1972) in Alameda County, California, studied children with listening (auditory perceptual) problems who were reading below grade level (also see Devine, 1967, and Duker, 1969). Lane and Miller (1972) found that listening instruction aided the reading of underachieving adolescents. Schneeberg (1977) found that students in grades one to six scored higher on standardized reading tests after they had participated in a broad program that included listening to the text of a book while they were reading it. (Also see Thomas and Rossiter, 1972, who used compressed listening to improve reading.)

Transfer of instruction from listening to reading may develop through improved attitudes of receiving, grasping the analogous features more securely, increasing common vocabulary skills, general improvement in memory and thinkings skills, and increased auditory perception, discrimination, and blending. But whether improvement comes from these elements or by some other means is usually unclear in the "shot gun" approaches of most studies.

There is speculation that improved reading comes with improved auditory discrimination,[3] which includes recognition of beginning sounds, final sounds, and vowel and rhyming or consonant sounds in words. Problems in discriminating may come from the following: (1) points of articulation, (2) degree of nasality, (3) amount of lip closure, and (4) voicing and unvoicing (e.g., /s/ representing a whispered or voiceless sound and /z/ representing a voiced sound with vibrations of the vocal chords).

Hearing difficulties may accompany reading difficulties. (For a review of research and discussion on auditory perception in reading, see Russell and Fea, 1963; Harris, 1969; Conrad, 1972; and Roswell and Natchez, 1977.) Children with only minor auditory deficiencies may find it difficult to hear certain sounds represented by such letters as *h,* even when they are close to the speaker. Such a deficiency may produce phonic difficulties—the recoding of sound-letter correspondence in reading. A child may need to hear words as composed of initial, middle, and final sounds *on occasion.* To grasp the idea that a word is composed of somewhat distinct yet *blended* sounds is usually foreign to beginners, for example, that the word *act* is blended—/ă→ăc→a+c+t→ăct/ or /ăkt/. A child may occasionally find it useful to discriminate syllables and word parts, as *spi* in spider.[4]

Auditory Discrimination

The logical conclusion is that children with an ear experienced in many voice and speech variations (including distinct pronunciation and articulation) have an advantage in that part of the reading process that unlocks words. The children who have "educated ears" may have a better idea of the extreme subtleties of word beginnings and endings in oral discourse than do those without (for example, "amusing" or "am using"). Yet even a child from an academically oriented environment may have trouble in hearing the separation of words. For example, when a child is saying the usual prayers at night, he or she might finally ask, "What does 'fieshudie' mean?" (Translation: "If I should die. . . .").

Wide experience, which includes exposure to different and varied dialects, overtones, and voice levels, usually gives background help to readers. Experience also provides direction where there are similar sound patterns but a different meaning. Even skillful secondary students may have trouble applying instructions in speaking a foreign language they are studying if they have heard only the model of their teacher's voice. Opportunities for auditory discrimination are useful in many areas. The responsibility for analyzing and organizing a stream of sounds into a series of words falls almost invariably to the listener, who must extract meaningful information from the sensations.

How is instruction and development as an accurate listener and reproducer of language directly linked with beginning success in reading? Unless the instructor helps children call on their listening background, it is unlikely that they will successfully attend to significant, specific sounds of words and word parts during reading. Variation in guided experiences and in obtaining a background for sounds is a factor contributing to differences in readiness for reading instruction. We need, however, to keep in mind that discriminated sounds are not the significant part of language; meanings are. This generalization applies to our stance on reading instruction. Mechanics of word recognition and pronunciation are not the significant part of reading; understanding meaning is. This bears repeating many times.

Stark (1957) has reviewed research on pupil ability to perform well on tests of isolated components of perceptual processing, including auditory, and the ability to perform the whole task of interpreting spoken or written language. He finds that the evidence is essentially not supportive of an individual skills training approach to learning disabilities:

> Some of the research we have cited suggests that children with reading failures need to learn the rules of spoken language. They need to develop strategies for processing morphophonemic and syntactic units [word sound and sentence units] and learn the logic of language systems. The efficacy of training so-called "word-attack" skills, teaching sound and letter correspondences, blends, and improving perceptual motor abilities must be questioned. (p. 833)[5]

Comparative thinking about listening and reading calls to mind teachers of students who do not speak standard English. Such teachers need to be familiar with each child's auditory discrimination in order to individualize instruction. Confusing for the teacher are omissions, additions, distortions, and substitutions in the sounds of what we call standard (or national network) English that may be associated with difficulties in auditory discrimination. But a child's apparent errors may relate to the sounds of the child's own dialect and nonstandard usage, or to both. For example, when a child says, "Ee 'it me" for "He hit me," is it dialect, discrimination, or defective hearing that prompts the omissions? Additional examples: a child might say "Joe is no here" (difficulty with negatives because of his or her dialect?), or "She a baby" for "She is [or she's] a baby" (difficulty with the present tense of verbs or with hearing?).

In "Black Children and Reading," Johnson and Simons (1972) suggest that when children read *kill* for *killed* or *pass* for *passed*, they may not know that the past tense has been signaled. The teacher must determine if the child needs to learn that *-ed* is an indicator of the past tense. But if listening and reading comprehension are not impaired, beginners will usually experience more security and comfort if they can impose their own sound systems on the standard English spelling in school reading materials. Essentially, children translate or recode standard English into their own dialect. A teacher should respect a child's reading of *He going* for *He is going* as long as there is comprehension.

There are sounds in black dialect that are systematically substituted for particular standard English sounds. For example, if a word ends in two consonant sounds and the last is /b/, /d/, /k/, /p/, or /t/, the last consonant is reduced or omitted; that is, *test* becomes *tes, desk* becomes *des, lift* become *lif,* and *killed* becomes *kill* (Johnson and Simons, 1972). Grammatical system is found in omissions of *is, am, are* in the present progressive tense: e.g., "He looking at me."

Some dialects create a shock when would-be readers see so many different endings for words they pronounce more or less alike. For example, if final consonant sounds /t/, /d/, /r/, and /l/ are weak or missing, then *fat, fad, far,* and *fall* are all pronounced, with only slight variations, as *fa.* Black, Chinese, and Japanese children who are exposed mainly to nonstandard English dialects may need listening and speaking activities that deal with attending to both word meaning and to the sounds of consonants, for example, in the middle of words (/r/, l/l/, as in ca*r*ry, a*l*ways) and in final positions (as in abou*t*, di*d*, blac*k*, hi*s*, fa*r*, du*r*ing). Informal observation that especially notes those words and their sounds that are consistently troublesome to the child during reading instruction can provide teachers with cues for individual practice needs. But the chances are that most children can recode successfully and do not need such practice. Children can understand and read standard English without speaking it (Hall and Freedle, 1973; also see Norton and Hodgson, 1974, and Gantt, Wilson, and Dayton, 1974–1975, who caution about, and question the need for and the appropriateness of, dialect materials).

If practice you must, it is advisable that the words and sounds be in the child's listening and speaking vocabulary, be interesting, and be those that are frequently used and are fairly consistent in the match between letter and sound. An example of an "interesting word" which can stimulate reading is the case of a severely retarded student who was asked to tell his favorite word. It happened to be *motor*. After sounding, tracing, saying, and writing this word, the student was asked, "Suppose you were going to make a manual for someone like me who knew nothing of motors. What would be the first thing you'd say?" The student responded, "Lift the hood." This oral expression became not only the first page of his own "book," but also the beginning of extensive progress in reading (adapted from Jeanette Veatch, *Individualized Reading,* Listener In-Service Cassette Library, Hollywood, California, 1971). Use of nonsense words, such as *aps,* or infrequent words, such as *asp,* simply because they illustrate the deletion and changing of sound placement in such words as *caps,* does not fit the requirements of interest and frequency. To avoid boredom, frustration, and waste of time, activity should be provided on the basis of individual diagnosis and need rather than as rote exercises going on and on as ends in themselves. Teacher X's class, where all the children are chanting in unison words that begin with the same sound ("monkey"–"mouse, moon, money, mother") every year in the third week of school, probably fails to meet individual needs.

Teachers must maintain a proper perspective on activity designed to develop auditory discrimination. Again, readers usually have so much meaning, context, and grammatical content helping them that they are relatively independent of letter-sound information. "A little dab will do you" is an expression that usually fits the amount of practice in auditory discrimination (phonics) that a child needs for reading. Such auditory practice is more useful to the child in spelling than in reading.

Balanced against the idea of a place for at least some school guidance in auditory discrimination is, again, the crowning idea of *meaning.* To repeat: in the last analysis, sounds heard are not the significant part of language; ultimately, meanings are the significant part, and this generalization applies to reading. Mechanics of word recognition and pronunciation are not the significant part of reading; meaning is—meaning derived from complex, extended discourse. To simply "bark" letter signs for certain sounds is neither reading nor speaking; this "barking" may represent going from a sound code to a print code, but it does not always indicate comprehension. If a child "barks out" the sounds "If . . . you . . . look . . . under . . . this . . . sign . . . you will . . . find . . . a . . . five . . . dollar . . . bill . . . and . . . you . . . keep . . . it" and then, uninformed, wanders away none the wiser or richer, she or he has failed to read—according to the present definition.

The most helpful role that listening can play in reading for meaning probably lies in a broad, general background of listening comprehension, more so than in specific auditory discriminations for isolated sounds. Thus, long periods of auditory discrimination practice with drill materials, including such mechanical aids as earphones, are not nearly as effective as face-to-face communication between teacher and child.[6] This most productive background rests on empathy, projective interpretation, and reactive abilities in listening (including creative problem solving).

For example, a child might say:

> I thought you said "junk" instead of "jump," and that's why I read it that way. I wasn't trying to be smart with you. Do you understand?

Reading and Listening: Summary Suggestions

The foregoing section has shown the associations between listening and reading, an area of great interest to educators. What does this interrelationship imply for classroom activity in general? Summarized below are some ideas about the relationship of listening to reading falling under the following topics: (1) readiness for school learning; (2) a relaxed social situation; (3) units of comprehension; (4) common or analogous signals; and (5) critical and emotional aspects (see Sticht, 1974).

Readiness. Both listening and reading instruction require attention to readiness for learning, including:

Experience with the English language

A speaking and listening vocabulary sufficient for the task

Evidence of interest in or positive feelings for language activity

Ability to remember and follow short sequences

Some children begin their schooling with well-developed listening abilities. Some are more ready for listening instruction than for reading instruction. A few need practice in simple, more global listening activities and concept attainment, such as whether or not sounds are the same or different, near or far, high or low, loud or soft, fast or slow. To illustrate more specifically, some teachers fill boxes with objects that rattle (such as peas, beads, shells, tacks, paper clips) and invite pairs of children to play discrimination games.[7]

Relaxed social situation. Both listening and reading flourish in a relaxed social situation where the ideas and language in spoken and written material are at least partly familiar to the child. To illustrate, some teachers provide familiar hats and costumes for a play corner. They then record the children's conversations via tape and transcribe them for reading material. One enterprising teacher created an enticingly relaxed social situation for reading by painting an old cast-iron bathtube orange, throwing in some cushions, and declaring it a reading center. She imposed three rules: no more than three in the tub, keep reading, no splashing. There was not a moment, from the opening of school to its close, that the tub was not filled with readers.

Units of comprehension. For both listening and reading, the sound or even the word is not the unit of language comprehension, but sounds or words do affect the meaning of phrases, sentences, paragraphs, and larger units of discourse (an example of a word affecting meaning: "I can't take my *eyes* off of you" versus "I can't take my spies off of you"). The unit of comprehension, however, is more likely to be the sentence, the paragraph, and the whole unit of discourse in context and in the varied relationships of ideas. (Here is an example of need for a larger context: "We are in support of striking Afghan hemp workers." Does the message mean "hitting" or does it mean "Afghans who refuse to work"?) An instructor who grasps the principle of large units of meaning connected with grammatical and literary patterns is careful to provide classroom activity related to complete language products, among them, original stories, dramatizations, children's literature (to tempt, inform, and delight), and other relevant and exciting products of child language. The understanding teacher uses these sources rather than a steady diet of isolated, drill-type exercises.

Common, analogous signals. Both listening and reading use signals, such as pauses and intonation for oral language and their corresponding punctuation marks for written language. Here is a classic example of the use of a pause corresponding to punctuation and to related changes of meaning in reading: "What's that in the road /,/ ahead?"

Critical thinking and emotional aspects. Both listening and reading may take place in either individual or social situations, but sometimes with varying effects. Research shows that both the analytical and the critical thinking processes may flourish better in the individual reading situation. A person is, for instance, more cautious when reading a propagandistic selection in a quiet room than when he or she receives the same message delivered orally to a group.[8] In contrast, appreciative, emotional, and creative reactions may flourish under the stimulus of a lively group situation. For example, a group of listeners gets more enjoyment and sensitive interpretation from a choral reading of the poem "John Brown's Body" than does an isolated listener. Because of the listener's greater susceptibility during group participation, however, teachers should put special learning emphasis on critical thinking during the *listening* situation. It is important to remember that powerful motivation for reading takes place during an intimate sensitive, and pleasing oral presentation to a group (see Devine, 1978).

How Does Listening Resemble Speaking?

Listening resembles speaking because both have a common code, draw on the same background, and have, in many cases, a common vocabulary. Both listening and speaking use a code of sound instead of print, and speech used resembles speech consistently heard. It follows that the words in a child's speaking vocabulary are also part of her or his listening vocabulary. However, a child may be able to use a difficult word in speech or in writing and understand it while listening and reading, but not know it in isolation.

An example is the word *confiscate,* used in the classroom context of removing forbidden objects such as gum, candy, and knives. Although children might meaningfully hear it and speak it, they might not be able to read it or to write it. Thus, words children know well enough to understand when used by another (listening vocabulary) may *not* be in their speaking or reading vocabularies, even if they are skilled in simply sounding out words without attaching meaning. (Relevant to this idea, see Cazden's 1966 review of cultural differences in children's language.)

Figure 2 illustrates the third element in the comparison of listening and speaking (and also reading and writing)—vocabulary. Four overlapping vocabularies are illustrated, the usual direction of development (depicted by arrows), and the relative size and overlapping of the listening vocabulary. What does this interrelationship imply for teachers? Simply that teachers need to concentrate on listening and speaking vocabularies before they anticipate competence and performance in written vocabulary. It means that teachers should read challenging stories each day to the children and in other ways provide a stimulating, rich, and varied listening diet (for young children see, for example, Cullinan and Carmichael, 1977). It means that teachers should encourage children to demand the meaning of the words they encounter and to be conscious of word meanings. That is, once children know the meaning of a new word in their listening vocabulary, teachers should help them to use it in their speaking, reading, and writing vocabularies.

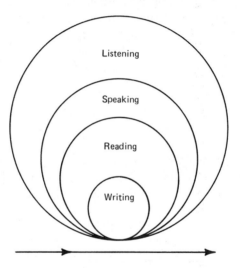

Fig. 2. Four overlapping vocabularies in the elementary school. Arrow indicates movement through time.

Another relationship in the listening-speaking dimension is distortion (Stammer, 1977). Teachers should examine distortions that commonly occur while children are listening to a spoken message, for they create differences between messages sent and messages received. Four distortions might be labeled: (1) attitude cutoff, (2) motive attribution, (3) organizational mix-up, and (4) self-preoccupation.

Attitude cutoff. This distortion cuts information off at the spoken source because attitude acts on selection. For example, if Jane has a strong negative reaction every time she hears the word *test,* she might not hear the rest of this message, "The test of any person lies in action." Readers and especially listeners often receive what they expect to, rather than what the original message-giver intended (Ammon, 1969).

Motive attribution. The second possible distortion, the attempt to attribute a motive to the speaker, might be illustrated by one who says, "He is just selling me a public relations line for the Establishment," or by a child who thinks, "Teachers just like to talk; they don't really expect me to listen the first time because they are going to repeat those directions ten times anyway."

Organizational mix-up. A third distortion may arise during message organization—"Did she say, 'Turn left, then right, then right, then left' or. . . ?" "Did he say, 'tired' or 'tried'?"

Self-preoccupation. A fourth distortion may occur when listeners become preoccupied with the message they want to formulate and then send back; for example, "I'll get him for that; as soon as he stops talking, I'll make a crack about how short he is, then . . ."

Preoccupation with his or her own message is a frequent distortion imposed by the young listener. Since memory span is tenuous, hanging on to one's own thoughts during communication takes a great deal of attention and energy. Some teachers help by suggesting that the young listeners make a small, quick picture to help cue their ideas when their turn arrives, which enables them to get back to listening. Older children may jot down "shorthand" notes to help them hold on to ideas until they return to the line of communication.

Throughout all of this cognitive and affective activity, irrational and unconscious attitudes are being reinforced, weakened, or changed. Attitudes, which may not be the same as those held by the speaker, are determining the meaning in the mind of the listener. There is a long, tortuous trail between speaking and listening in the communication act. The listener "creates" the language of the speaker. Thus, while the message is ideally the same for the speaker and for the listener, contrasts are usually present (also see Stammer, 1977).

How Does Listening Resemble Writing?

In the communication diagram (Figure 3), listening is represented as the most distant from and thus the least like writing, which is an expressive process transmitting to the sense of sight. However, speaking and writing, as skills of transmission, do have some common elements; but listening and reading are skills of reception. Moreover, people rarely speak in the same manner they write—from the standpoint of sound, grammar, tonal patterns, and vocabulary. Example: they say "winshiel" but write "windshield."

But there are associations between listening and writing, such as the internal listening that accompanies writing and the already mentioned common background, including vocabulary. When children are composing ideas in written form, they speak and listen internally as they record: "Let's see, I'm going to write about a dog that ate a mean man. . . No, let's make it a woman . . ."[9] Since listening is a foundation for writing, improving listening is likely to affect composition. However, improvement may not be immediately apparent because of complexity, the slow pace of such growth, and the imprecision in measurement of language arts skills.

Another influence of listening on writing is the careful discrimination, observation, and translation into sensory images of sounds that a writer may describe. Use of vivid auditory imagery to help the reader experience a setting is one of the tools of writing, as when a writer sets a mood by noting the plaintive chirp of a cricket. (Lasser, 1973, had students watch a film run without sound, write scripts for it, then run the film and compare the scripts.)

Finally, there is evidence of dependence obtained from studies of deaf children who lag considerably behind hearing children in writing skill (Cooper, 1965). Studies reveal that compositions of the deaf, which show less unity in style, less variety, and less use of probability, resemble those of hearing children about three years younger. Hearing children use more compound and complex sentences with a greater number of verbs in the clauses. The deaf show practically no increase in "clause use" with age (Heider and Heider, 1940; Cooper, 1965). To be deaf, to be confined to the lonely, limited world of silence, may be more emotionally disabling than blindness (Ratcliff, 1971). Thus, writing is both directly and indirectly dependent upon listening.

How does the relationship between listening and writing affect classroom activity? First, children must be free to talk aloud and listen to themselves while they write. They need to receive oral feedback on their ideas before, during, and after they write (Conrad, 1971; Graves, 1974; Vygotsky, 1962). Graves (1974) found that seven year olds (boys especially) need to mutter to themselves, talk an idea out through a series of pictures, and listen to themselves before and during the composition sequences.

Summary

In this chapter listening has been compared and related to speaking, reading, and writing. In Figure 3 listening is placed in the upper lefthand corner to represent a beginning position because listening vocabularies are normally learned first. Since listening (or any language art) is not a watertight compartment, arrows denote interaction with the other language arts. Notice, too, the discrimination of the language pair for receiving messages (denoted by placement together on the left) and the language pair for *expressing* (denoted by placement on the right).[10]

For the sake of illustration, take a child named Ted, who is moving through the stages illustrated in Figure 3. He *listens* to his name being called for a game, or he *reads* it on the class chart, which lists the order of turns. In both cases he *receives* a message. This type of act is represented by the lefthand side of the diagram. If, in response, Ted then moves over to the game center of the classroom, observers are reasonably sure of his reception of the message, and if he hears no remonstrance that he has done the wrong thing, he has increased assurance of his own reception.

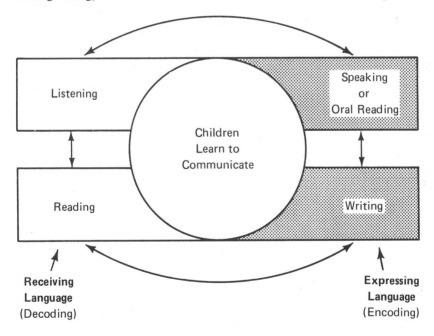

Fig. 3. Listening compared to the other language arts. Arrows denote the constant interaction among the language arts, with communication at the core.

He has adequately used the skills on the receiving side of the diagram.

However, Ted might be *speaking* the name of a game player (calling it out), or *writing* the name on the chart. In both cases he is *expressing* a message. If the appropriate child responds, an observer may be reasonably sure that Ted has expressed himself adequately, as represented on the communication diagram. But if Ted, as receiver or expresser, did not originally hear and comprehend the sound symbols that represent the name (listening background), it is doubtful that any kind of communication would take place.

A balanced program based on this diagram slights none of the mutually reinforcing arts of language. Since listening has been gravely slighted in instructional programs of the past, this chapter has been devoted to its analysis by comparing and contrasting it with the other language arts—speaking, writing, and reading.

A final word—it is obvious that the integrated language arts program is a program in language and thinking. The receiving sections of the language arts, reading and listening, support thinking by making use of skillfully acquired information. Not all problems are solved by using effective listening and reading, but it is doubtful that many are solved without help from these subskills. Listening is a crucial beginning link in the chain of subskills. This statement is another way of defining listening and putting it into proper perspective—as a subskill to productive, creative problem solving (Lundsteen, 1976a).

2 What Occurs During Proficient Listening?

The last chapter, by using a comparative definition to approach listening, established the following: (1) instruction in listening can enhance speaking, writing, and reading; (2) listening is a basic underlying skill, not only for the other language arts but also for creative problem solving; and (3) the relationship between auditory discrimination and reading is observed (sometimes unduly) in the schools. Granted, auditory discrimination is an important step in the listening process as educators know it, but what about the steps before and after auditory discrimination? What clues aid the child in following the other steps in listening?

This chapter presents the major divisions and steps that a proficient listener may take—a structural definition. It asks the question: "What are the parts of listening?" This organization will help the reader to identify what is teachable in listening and will serve as a framework for further ideas. This chapter considers the problems that children may encounter along the way, how to screen for them, and what a teacher can do about them. "What-to-do" often takes the form of illustrative games. Part of the teacher's problem in providing listening instruction has been the lack of a careful analysis of what a skilled listener does. Thus, one of the most important and helpful teaching concepts developed here is based upon the distinctions between hearing and listening and attention and listening. Use these distinctions as a checklist to ferret out children's problems and successes and to ensure that your listening program is balanced.

What Are the Parts of Listening and How Do They Function?

Five components of listening emerge from most analyses. They are:

1. Previous knowledge
2. Listening material
3. Physiological activity (hearing, sensation, perception)

4. Attention or concentration

5. Highly conscious, intellectual activity at the time of listening and beyond

These components are considered in the remainder of this chapter. The last three, physiological activity, attention, and intellectual activity, are analyzed further by breaking them down into ten steps that a proficient listener takes: (1) hear, (2) hold in memory, (3) attend, (4) form images, (5) search the past store of ideas, (6) compare, (7) test the cues, (8) recode, (9) get meaning, and (10) intellectualize beyond the listening moment.

This presentation may seem overly complex, but if the child does not go through all of these steps, the one that is missed may signal the point at which her or his communication is breaking down. Moreover, as each step is presented, it will become clear that many of them also apply to the reading process.

The entire definitional framework is shown, in outline form, in Figure 4. While each step is taken in a given listening act, they do not necessarily occur in a rigid, set order. There is much over-lapping, circling back, and almost simultaneous occurrence among them. The first two parts of the outline, previous knowledge and material, are examined in detail below. Without them, listening activity cannot proceed.

Previous Knowledge

An important component of listening is the background that a listener brings to the encounter. Background may include facts, ideas, rules, principles, attitudes, values, beliefs, and language base (including grammar, meaning, and vocabulary). If listeners lack the background to understand the message, they can still accomplish intake physiologically, but they will not be able to listen with comprehension.

For example, if you are a visitor from one region of the nation to another, you might say, "I believe I'll *crack* the window a bit" (meaning—open it). But you may get a horrified look from the uninformed listener (unaccustomed to your regional dialect), who might infer that you are going to break it. In addition, if a teacher lacks the background to know, for example, that "unzip the pine top" means "making the teacher back down," he or she may hear the message but fail to have the required knowledge to compre-hend these verbal symbols—that is, to listen with understanding.

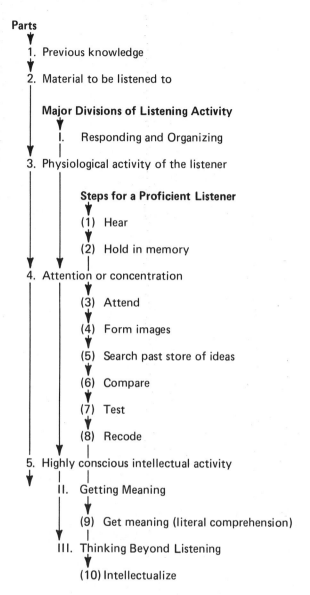

Parts

1. Previous knowledge

2. Material to be listened to

   Major Divisions of Listening Activity

   I.   Responding and Organizing

3. Physiological activity of the listener

   Steps for a Proficient Listener

   (1) Hear

   (2) Hold in memory

4. Attention or concentration

   (3) Attend

   (4) Form images

   (5) Search past store of ideas

   (6) Compare

   (7) Test

   (8) Recode

5. Highly conscious intellectual activity

   II. Getting Meaning

   (9) Get meaning (literal comprehension)

   III. Thinking Beyond Listening

   (10) Intellectualize

Fig. 4. An outline for a definition of listening.

Does lacking a store of specific pieces of information mean that the teacher in the example about the "pine top" was stupid, thinks illogically, has other language meanings of possibly more value than these? Such derogatory and misguided inferences are applied to those children who are linguistically different and who have been labeled disadvantaged, deprived, disprivileged, culturally different. But these children may have quick, agile minds, well equipped to handle the logic of survival, for example, in the ghetto. Their language may have meanings of intricate, subtle complexity. Consider these examples of linguistic ability shown in the private speech of the ghetto child: broken homes are "trees without roots"; outsiders coming in looking for thrills are "tops on a fairy lake"; being in trouble is expressed as "flying backward" (Brewer, 1966). Another example of vivid analogy is a black child's lament over the gang activity of some of his friends of which he was innocent but suffered guilt by association: "You know, they left me a mighty heavy coat to wear!" However, such children may indeed fail to appreciate the "funny, funny!" caption of a picture in a school reader of a cat that has just spilled the milk. This reaction is especially true when the child projects that this could be the only milk that the cat would see again for a long time. Listeners are flexible and have some tolerance for variations in dialect and context. But generally, without an appropriate background, listening as meaningful communication collapses.

One of the best ways to check children's previous knowledge is to ask if each one can tell, in his or her own words, what you mean. As you get this feedback, you either move forward or take time to build needed background. Such action seems obvious, but it is surprisingly neglected in many classrooms.

To illustrate the behavior of a proficient listener, visualize a living room setting where there is a foreign-born guest whose English varies from standard pronunciation. His communication represents a challenge to the host, who is a fairly proficient listener with respect to his own background and dialect. This continuing illustration tracks listener activity as it relates to each one of the parts and the ten steps that follow.

Continuing illustration. In this example, the host-listener is lacking a background for translating (or recoding) one pronunciation of a word into a variation. Background of this sort is useful in certain classrooms, especially in those where children speak other languages or dialects.

Listening Material

Background plays an important part in the listening act, but so does the material or the message. If we eliminated all messages, there would not be any listening. The word *auding* is more accurate here than *listening* because auding refers to comprehension of the material on which the speech symbol is based. Listening, a more general term, refers to reception of any kind of sound.[1]

Continuing illustration. The communicant from the foreign country suddenly sends his host material in the form of an oral message interpreted as, "Do I see a cot?" This is a simple question, but it should be remembered because it is used to trace the parts of listening and the steps taken by a proficient listener during the rest of the chapter.

Modifications in communication range from a single aural symbol such as "Oh!" to the use of many symbols with complex, multiple meanings. Consider this example: "I-know-you-believe-you - understood - what - you - think - I - said, but - I - am - not - sure - you - realize - that - what - you - heard - is - not - what - I - meant." The message may be speeded up, slowed down, or masked by noises or competing messages (such as the sound track from the film shown in the next classroom).[2] The message may be monotonous, such as a child's social studies report read in a droning voice directly from an encyclopedia. Or it may contain much variation in tone, pitch, quality, and structure. It may have clear signals made up of pauses and intonations similar to punctuation in printed matter, or the spoken signals may be unclear, as in the possibly cynical "They are trying to help him, *out*!" It may have a tight, logical organization (questions and overviews, as illustrated in this chapter). Or it may be disorganized, as in the incoherent account of a child who has just seen a tightrope artist plunge to earth. The message may elicit strong emotional reactions (as was possible with the tightrope disaster), or the response may be even weaker than it is in reading (as in a casual request to "pass the salt"). It may be highly listenable (parallel to readable), as in a recounting by one child to another of the tightrope incident several weeks later. Or it may be low in listenability for most hearers, as in the scientific recounting of the incident by a researcher interested in the physics of falling bodies. In this last case the message may employ technical jargon couched in involved sentence structures (see Glasser, 1975).

Messages may have linguistic structures: letter-sound (or graphophonological), sentence (or syntactic), and meaning (or semantic). This nonsense example is an illustration: "Neglands stregorize frozily." Although the specifics of this sentence do not give any *meaning,* listeners can probably accept the letter-sound structure if they hear it and repeat it aloud. They can probably get some sentence sense because the first word bears noun characteristics hinging upon its position in the sentence. Also the first word, "neglands," has the *s* on the end, suggesting that the word refers to more than one in a class. The next word, ending in *-ize,* suggests a verb form; the last word, ending in *-ily,* hints of quality because of the ending and the position of the word in the sentence.

Usage and types of discourse also make an impact on the material. The aims of the message sender also affect the definition of and work with, not only listening but the other language arts as well. Frequently, a message can be classified as emphasizing one of these aims:

Self-expression (personal, emotive)

Expository (reference oriented or informative, including the exploratory, the scientific)

Literary (e.g., poetic, dramatic, narrative)

Persuasive (incitive, designed to influence)

For example, return momentarily to the continuing illustration of the host and his foreign guest, who asked the question interpreted as "Do I see a cot?" The guest was most probably using the expository aim of communication, but he may have had a merely self-expressive aim.

Material requires various *channels* in order to reach the listener. These channels have an impact not only on the material but also on the receiver. Some channels, such as face-to-face, provide for fuller communication than do others. According to McLuhan, the "medium is the message"; that is to say, media impose various restrictions that either contribute to or hinder the reception of a message. These media (such as TV, telephone, radio, and tape recorder) involve contacts ranging from an individual to a small group, a large group to a mass audience. Group size introduces another possible influence on the material, but the fullest use of a channel occurs in the face-to-face encounter. Person-to-person communication may use not only the acoustical (i.e., sound waves) parts of speech as a channel, but also some of the following elements: (1) paralinguistic qualifiers, such as tone of voice, tempo, humming, and snorting; (2) such nonvocal bodily movements as hand gestures, raised eyebrows, and shrugs of the shoulders;[3] (3) touch and chemical-electrical possibilities; and (4) most important of all, feedback. Such media as the telephone, radio, tape, and TV, which mainly use the listening or acoustical channel, are lacking one or more of the preceding four possible components in the face-to-face situation with feedback opportunities.

How does this discussion apply to our everyday lives? We all need to listen to a variety of data just as much as we need to eat a variety of foods in our meals. Otherwise, we are prone to seek a steady diet of easy and unchallenging material, such as mindless gossip. When children hear something different, they can be challenged to analyze it, whether that something different is a dramatic presentation of children's literature or a nature study. In the best situations, what children hear in the classroom provides opportunities to become flexible and skilled in listening.[4]

A research study by Chomsky (1972) supports the possible lifting effect of a challenging listening diet. High complexity in the material read aloud to children was found to be closely associated with the degree of skill in comprehending complex sentence structures used in speaking to children five to ten years of age. Also see Klinzing (1972), who found that simplifying spoken syntactic structure in speaking to preschool children did not facilitate their decoding ability, but it did tend to retard their encoding ability.

The deficiencies of various channels and media (telephone, TV) may make it necessary for teachers to use material designed to take into account the several dialectical and ethnic groups in their classrooms. Teachers can help children cope with differences in material when the speaker is not present or *is* present—that is when there is a chance to ask questions, be interactive, and exploit an opportunity for review. (See the work of Di Vesta on note-taking and listening, e.g., Di Vesta and Gray, 1972-1973).

There is more to the speaker context of material that applies to the classroom. Even elementary school children can be helped to realize the effect on themselves of "people" context during listening situations. "People context" might include the following (from Ostermeir, 1967): (1) the relative authority level of the speaker ("mighty teacher"—or "just a lowly pupil"); (2) self-reference in order to increase credibility ("I saw it with my own eyes!"); (3) prestige reference to increase trustworthiness ("My dad says . . . ," "The president says . . . ," "Teacher says . . .").

In (1) above, the relative authority level of the speaker, consider the role it plays in the classroom. To illustrate, some teachers fail to pay much attention not only to children's spoken words, but also to their various nonverbal, physical reactions. But how children watch for these small signs (such as the drumming of fingers) in their teachers! However, some teachers do pay enormous attention to all elements of communication from people in authority—such as principal, consultant, superintendent of schools. In essence, some children seem to be more careful about watching teachers' reactions than some teachers seem to be about watching those of the children. But for the program and learning suggested in this book, the progression of attending demands careful teacher awareness. Cues should be taken from a wide variation of pupil behavior and teaching should be adjusted accordingly. Analyze your nonverbal behavior via videotape camera as you send listening material to children. Remember, a high level of authority with little awareness and solicitation of feedback may be a silencer of children's needed communication.

Responding and Organizing

According to the outline for a definition of listening (Figure 4), the next task is to move from "previous knowledge" and "material" to major divisions of listener activity. The first broad division, responding and organizing, includes the third structural part, physiological activity. It includes two steps: (1) hearing and (2) holding in memory, which will be discussed shortly.

Physiological Activity of the Listener

The physiological activity that centers on hearing is that part of the listening act that takes us into a series of steps for proficient listening. First, sound waves are received by the ear in what may be raw, undifferentiated sensory experience. The two steps covered in this section include (1) hear and (2) hold in memory. The first step, hear, consists of four components: auditory acuity, discrimination (dealt with in the last chapter), analysis, and sequencing. This detailed analysis of the step makes possible an important distinction between mere hearing and actual listening.

Step 1: Hear

The listener starts the act by hearing a speech sound or series of symbols. The speaker has uttered these sounds by using, for example, levels of loudness (volume) from a certain distance, at a certain speed, with a particular enunciation, at a certain pitch (frequency), timbre (sound-wave form), in the combinations of these that influence the intelligibility of the material. The listener *accumulates* this sound. She or he receives a word over a brief interval of time, collecting bit by bit.

Continuing illustration. To illustrate this first step (and all of the components we will assign to it), consider again the example of the foreign-born visitor and his listening host. The visitor seemed to say, "Do I see a cot?" The listening host hears with the necessary acuity, accumulates sound, discriminates one sound from the other, and analyzes and sequences this message. But he is nonetheless puzzled as there is apparently no "cot" in the room.

Although the listening host may not realize it, he is now calling upon his ability to perceive speech despite distortion of his own dialect. Unconsciously, he has also probably dissected the words and the grammatical structure of this sentence. He may have concluded (unconsciously) that the message is a question containing a subject, a transitive verb, and an object. In other words, this hearing step, as well as some of the others, includes basic linguistic competence. While word order is no problem for him, nor is intonation, in no shape, form, or substance can he see a cot!

To assign so much activity to the hearing step may be misleading. It is time to make a distinction between hearing and listening. Hearing refers to the conversion of pressure waves into neural impulses moving to the brain. There, the process of auditory perception and listening with interpretation may begin. Compare the part of the physiological activity called hearing with the seeing or reception of vibrations of light in reading. Neither hearing nor seeing implies formation or comprehension of an idea. But of course accurate hearing must come before accurate, interpretive listening. Listening includes more conscious activity of the mind than does mere hearing. In the continuing host-listener example, the host has heard his guest's message, but he himself doubts that he has listened because a word fails to make sense to him.

This distinction between hearing and listening has important implications for instruction. Just because a child has heard a given direction does not mean he or she has listened to it. Sometimes teachers who equate the two processes wonder why children are disobedient and obstinate when they are not really so.

Next, examine four components of this hearing step: (1) auditory acuity (degree of hearing loss, if any); (2) discrimination (determining likenesses or differences in sound); (3) analysis (largely an unconscious "taking apart" in response to pitch, tone, and rhythm); and (4) auditory sequencing (recall of sound in proper time order). An examination of these components as they relate to screening for problems follows. Each component is illustrated with classroom games. If a listener is deficient in any one of these components of the hearing step, his or her ability to listen suffers.

Auditory acuity refers to the reception of sound waves of various tones at various levels of loudness (amplitude). Acuity also determines the degree of efficiency of the hearing organs. There is a parallel between amplitude in listening and the brightness or dimness of the printed symbol in reading.[5]

Probably 5 to 10 percent of children are handicapped in auditory acuity, such as a temporary hearing loss caused by infected tonsils or adenoids. These handicaps may determine the amount of sound picked up and the shape of the resonance chambers. Consequently, the resultant input changes may confuse the child. Children with inadequate housing and medical care may also be prone to respiratory ailments that affect the ears and may lose opportunities for learning auditory discriminations useful in reading and spelling.

How do you recognize the pupil who is hard of hearing? How does he or she react differently from the hearing child? You can watch for the child who cups his or her ear and leans forward to hear, who speaks too loudly or too softly, or who has trouble pronouncing words (i.e., slightly inarticulate speech). Watch for the child who has difficulty in rhyming words or in differentiating similar sounds. Another look at the child's school audiometer test may also be in order.[6] (Hopefully it was given early by competent personnel.) Auditory acuity may set the limits within which discrimination between likenesses and differences of sound operates, but there is no evidence that acuity guarantees discrimination (Harris, 1969). Young children who are hard of hearing will have intensified difficulty not only with softness of sounds, but also with distracting noise or competing messages. This problem is also intensified in minimally brain-damaged children.

In binaural hearing problems caused by a lack of coordinated functioning of both ears, a parallel can be drawn to disability in depth perception in seeing (vital, for instance, to a driver when judging distance in passing or to a catcher in grasping a high ball). Ability to identify an individual speaker among several speakers indicates properly functioning binaural hearing. But again, a basic difficulty makes for poor listening. Teachers can screen for binaural problems by asking the children to close their eyes and then to point to the location of noises made from various areas of the room.

Auditory discrimination, the ability to discriminate among sounds, was treated in the last chapter; hence, no further mention of this component is made here.

Auditory analysis, a requisite component of auditory discrimination, refers to the responses children may make to changes in pitch or tone, volume (intensity), and rhythm without being aware that they are doing so. Listeners use auditory analysis when they hear the sound sequences of an unfamiliar language or dialect. Analysis takes sounds apart, as in the separation of sounds in the word *sun* into *s—u—n;* synthesis puts sounds back together. When sounds are separated by as little as a second, synthesis becomes difficult, even for an adult (Witkin, 1969; Seymour, 1970). Both analysis and synthesis are important in the next component, sequencing. Blending exercises are examples of how teachers screen for problems in this area. Children who have problems with auditory analysis call attention to themselves during work with phonics in reading instruction and when listening to a word to be spelled ("libary" for "library").

Auditory sequencing refers to the recall of sounds in a proper time sequence. An illustration of this operation is the segmentation of language flow, such as "pleasesitdown" into "Please sit down." Closely related to the next step, auditory sequencing in its more complex forms is related to auditory memory and to the meaning of a sentence. Examples of sequence related to meaning are the differences between "The lion ate the tiger" and "The tiger ate the lion." "He went to bed and ate three banana splits" may not carry the same meaning as "He ate three banana splits and went to bed" (quite ill).

How would you recognize a listening problem in recalling sounds in proper time sequence—a major dimension of language? Jim, who has difficulty, may carry out only the last of several instructions, mix them up, or consistently garble the pronunciation of strange new words. He may mispronounce names, have difficulty in remembering the order of phone numbers, and transpose sounds. He may also fail to discriminate the sequence of auditory symbols in the directions "Melt butter in a pot; brown a large onion, add flour and curry." For the word "totem pole" he may be saying "temtopole" or "pesgetti" for "spaghetti."

Application

What games can the teacher use to develop these four components of the hearing step? Here are a few; more are given at the end of the chapter. When these games are used, encourage individual pupils to chart their successes for self-evaluation. Grade levels are specified in parentheses after each activity.

Scrambled eggs. Unscrambling sentences composed of words in random order is a game that can be used to test for auditory sequencing of extended discourse. For example: "Sky across the like marched clouds the giants" unscrambled would be "The clouds marched like giants across the sky." To make the task easier, underline the word that comes first when the sentence is arranged in grammatical order. Another example: "Like sound the I sail swift-slapping of a." Children can hold short sentences in memory and rearrange them orally; or they can number the words in sequence, cut and paste them, or rewrite the sentence. Here are other possibilities for unscrambling:

Barefoot floor across the chilly ran I

Wing way their butterflies white pale softly as a sigh long

Hovered horses sea a stabled in a cave green great

When you use the scrambled eggs game, select sentences that are interesting to your children and are worth their efforts to unscramble them. During this game children can also consciously discover something about how our language is put together grammatically, such as the order of adjectives. (Primary-intermediate) (See Russell and Russell, 1959, for other sequence games, such as "What shall we take on the picnic?")

Make your voice sound like this one. A game in which children try to make their voices sound like that of another person can aid in the development of auditory analysis and discrimination; it can also promote more pleasant voice qualities. In a related game, the child who is "it" covers her or his eyes while a teacher points to the child who is to read, in either a normal or funny voice, a syllable printed on a card. If "it" correctly guesses the reader, the child reading the syllable becomes "it." (Primary-intermediate)

Say me same. Read unfamiliar foreign language phrases (or play them from a recording) or use funny-sounding nonsense syllables ("ish-golish-metich") and ask the children to repeat them. Tape recording and playback can aid evaluation. (Primary-intermediate)

Step 2: Hold in Memory

Auditory memory is important for several reasons. If listeners are to judge whether or not two or more speech sounds are alike, they must keep the sounds in mind in order to retrieve them for comparison. They cannot make simultaneous comparisons in listening, as they can in reading, where they examine fixed letters; they have to depend upon their auditory memory. People also tend to convert visual information to a memory that is structured for sound by verbalizing to themselves. Effective listening probably rests on an adequate auditory memory span. An inadequate memory span indicates a possible cause not only of listening problems, but of reading difficulties as well (Harris, 1969).

Long-term and short-term memory are especially important when dealing with meaning, that is, recalling the attributes of a concept, such as "cot," heard and learned years ago. When working with children, the teacher may ask, "Has the material disappeared or has it become too buried in this child's mental storage files (long-term memory) or was it never stored in the first place (short-term memory)?" By rehearsing or repeating terms aloud to themselves, individuals can keep items in their short-term store, referred to aptly as "scratch pad" memory. But the number of items they can maintain there is limited, probably seven to nine digits. Once information is lost from the short-term store, it is irretrievable. But individuals can transfer it into their relatively permanent long-term memory by bringing to present mind the associations from the long-term store to be joined to the short-term information. For example, they can use a mnemonic device for remembering a name and a face, such as "Mr. Skinosski is a man who has a nose like a ski jump."

Teachers can try to help children retrieve information from the long-term store by the use of probes, similar to the way a classification system is used to find a book in the library so that it can be scanned for needed information. During a game, instead of trying to randomly recall states of the union beginning with the letter *M*, a child might better use a systematic probe, such as a geographic location. Such systematic strategies may take longer, but ultimately they are usually more successful and thorough. The more background of relevant experience children have (or that a teacher can help furnish), the more they can construct information from what they listen to (or read). For example, a chess master with an extensive chess background can remember twenty-five pieces from a board layout exposed for fifteen seconds, but beginners can recall only about seven pieces because they lack a background of organizational schemes that would enable them to recall more than individual pieces.

Continuing illustration. The host-listener has probably rehearsed several times to himself his guest's utterance, "Do I see a cot?" in an effort to retain this seemingly meaningless message. As he repeats the sentence using his short-term memory, he has probably succeeded in placing it in his long-term memory as he pulls out past associations with the words.

' When screening for difficulties in short-term auditory memory, a simple test is to tap a rhythm with a pencil, which the child then repeats. A teacher might check vowel and consonant short-term memory by asking a child to repeat a string of sounds, such as /a-too-a-op/. A few reading teachers find a high incidence of deficiency in the last listening steps (auditory analysis and discrimination, sequencing, and especially auditory memory) among minority group students who are successful in their use of visual skills. The key to unlocking further progress lies, for a few individuals, in enhancing auditory skills. The following is an example of a classroom activity related to memory.

Application

Control tower. Pupils pretend to be airplane pilots listening for landing instructions. They must hold these in memory and sequence them correctly to come in for a perfect landing. For example:

> How do I land?
> Fly around the library table, over to the third window, along the bookcases, circle the listening center three times, and come to rest under the pencil sharpener.

For long series, encourage children to use such devices as rehearsal, association, and organization. Have the children keep a record of their successes. (Primary)

Attention or Concentration

Attending (like physiological activity) is another part of the listening situation. The attending step (like memory) probably operates almost continually throughout all of the other steps.

Step 3: Attend

In this step listeners focus, concentrate, and select cues from the speech sounds. To use the analogy of a radio, they "tune in." Their selection of cues may depend upon the repetitions of the conversation and nonverbal gestures of the speaker. During attending, they may also need to follow the utterance (or track the sounds) through time. (It may take a listener one-third of a second to hear a syllable.) Their awareness includes recognizing that a sound has started, stopped, or changed. (See Stanners et al., 1972, on the pupilary response to variation in material.)

Continuing illustration. When the proficient listener in our living room scene heard his guest speaking to him, he probably attended, concentrated, focused, and selected sound against a background. This general noise level of sounds may have come from his stereo, the wind chimes on the balcony, a motorcycle in the parking lot below, the police helicopter, and the crash of a wave on the not-too-distant beach. Rarely do people deal with a single sound against a background of complete silence. They select specific sounds and ignore the rest. Two key components in the attending step are focus and selection.

Focus refers to the location of a sound source in relation to the listener. Babies turn their heads toward laughter from someone they cannot see. A teacher may use more advanced focusing to identify which child in a class of forty running on the playground used an unusual word. Selection, another component of the attention step, is related to such devices as an object that at first glance is apparently a white vase on a black background. But as the eye studies it, the design may turn into two black vases on a white background. This behavior is sometimes referred to as figure-ground distinction rather than selection.

The listener makes selections not only against a background of noise (as in the continuing illustration), but also from the stream of language. To phrase it linguistically, the user selects the most productive cues from surface structures, such as signals for the plural or the past tense. The language user can get to underlying structure and to language meaning, but avoid using every feature and relationship of every sound.

When, in the continuing illustration, the host heard the question "Do I see a *cot*?" he was probably giving special attention to the sounds and the rising intonation comprising the last puzzling word. Similarly, a child learning to read learns that some letters in a word are more important than others. For example, the initial consonant may carry more information as to a word's identity than do other letters (Samuels, 1969). If a child reads "Do I see a cot?" the chances are that the other sentences and picture would be redundant so he or she need attend only to the initial letter *c* and rapidly move on.

Selection from context cues (not trial and error) controls the order in which listeners try to match the message they reconstruct with the actual one. Many tentative identifications are made on the basis of what the listener expects from context.

Sometimes the terms *attend* and *concentrate* are misinterpreted as synonyms for listening. Yet a child can give his or her most earnest attention to a strange foreign language and still not comprehend, that is, listen. Listening is not only more than hearing, it is also more than attention. Attention is a necessary but not sufficient condition for learning from verbal materials. (An ear specialist, however, may find that more than half of proclaimed deafness is nothing more than inattention.)

The school environment sometimes discourages attention. Notably, business and industry have learned the importance of attention. They hold presentations that are designed to influence performance to not more than twenty minutes and take pains to minimize distraction, monotony, irritating gestures, and poor conditions; on the positive side, appropriate tone and organization are emphasized. It is not uncommon, however, for children to have to listen far beyond their reasonable attention spans. This they must do while lawn mowers clatter, other children shout outside the window, people walk on noisy flooring, and they sit in sweltering temperatures—in short, they encounter every imaginable kind of inhibition to attention. All of this distraction occurs in spite of the knowledge that two equally competing messages presented at the same time render each incomprehensible (Broadbent, 1962, 1966). The need to apply this information to the child's learning environment is long overdue. (Also see research by Doyle, 1973, on listening and distraction, a developmental study of selective attention. She found that superior child listeners inhibited their response to distracting information during the selection task, rather than filtering it out early.)

Application

A child who has difficulty in paying attention and in concentrating may fail to hear signals if the playground or classroom is especially noisy. Or she or he may be unable to follow the teacher's instructions if there is some class commotion or if there are distracting noises outside. You might test attention, awareness, and concentration by saying to a pupil, "Raise your hand when you hear an animal sound," or some other signal.

Children who are easily distracted may need guidance in gradually extending the time they can attend to messages. Thirty seconds, two minutes, five minutes of story time may eventually stretch to twenty minutes of attentive enjoyment. Easily distracted children may profit from using context clues to fill in those parts that their wandering attention has caused them to miss.

Context and rhyme appear in a game of attending to unfinished verse. For example, "Billy *Jones* cries and _____ (moans)," "Janie *Ling* will dance and _____ (sing)." Pupil partners can compete in composing and in attending to context. (Primary-intermediate)

A child with apparent difficulty in figure-ground discrimination or selection may need a simple classroom environment, visual as well as auditory, to facilitate listening, such as a "quiet" classroom. Children who have problems in tracking might find it helpful to talk relevantly to themselves; they can anticipate the message and work around it. If teachers of these children allow them to "talk their lessons" out loud to themselves, it might improve their concentration, attention, and learning processes (Graves, 1973; Vygotsky, 1962; Conrad, 1971).

The use of *compressed speech* in instruction may be the future answer to problems of attention in some cases.[7] The time lag between the speed of speech and the beginning of listening coupled with thinking causes attention to the message to waver. Thought may be ten times faster than speech. The leftover thinking space that is blank until the speaker's next words are uttered can get the unskilled listener into mischief. While normal speech may progress at the rate of 125 to 175 words per minute, speech speeded up to 350 words per minute shows little comprehension loss, depending on the material. In fact, blind people, who use speeded-up records and have acquired some skill in listening, prefer more acceleration in presentation than do sighted people (Duker, 1968; Sticht, 1969). Education in the future may employ speeded-up spoken discourse in order to increase consistency of attention and comprehension and to raise the rate of transmission of spoken information and its assimilation up to typical reading rates. *Expanded* speech, on the other hand, might be useful in the analysis and teaching of foreign languages.

A few additional classroom activities for promoting attending follow. Others are at the end of the chapter.

Hear it? Have the children close their eyes and listen for a given period of time. Then to a partner they tell or write everything they heard, such as a clock ticking, feet shuffling, leaves blowing, footsteps in the hall. Or the children might attend to the precise sound of rhythm band instruments, closing their eyes as each is played. Or, while the children listen to musical compositions, they can try to distinguish among the instruments. (Primary-intermediate)

Likely or unlikely? The leader tells about an action, and if the statement is likely (e.g., fish swim), the children raise their hands. If the statement is unlikely (trees swim), they keep their hands on their knees. The children should record individual successes in attending. Various school content areas may be used in this game. (Primary-intermediate)

Have you seen my friend? The leader says to a child, "Have you seen my friend?" Then that player responds, "How does he (or she) look?" The leader begins to describe one of the other players. As soon as the listener recognizes the child described, the listener tries to touch him or her. A chase around the circle may take place once. If the player who took the part of the listener does not succeed in touching the child described, then he or she becomes the describer. If the listener does touch the child described, then the tagged child becomes the describer. Others in the group pay attention in order to check on whether or not the description and choice are identifiable. (Primary-intermediate)

Step 4: Form Images

After attending, listeners form tentative images from the sound cues. During this step they may translate the sound image into internal speech. They may give to a word or message a meaning that probably includes an internal picture of the thing or event named by the word. The picture-evoking value of words can be a key to ease of learning. It may be even more important than frequency of use and meaningfulness.

The study of memory suggests two separate elements in auditory image formation: sound and meaning. Most errors in short-term memory arise from confusions between sounds, even when materials are presented to the sense of sight, e.g., "Was the word *can,* or was it *can't?*" Errors in short-term memory arising from confusion in meaning are relatively rare, yet in long-term memory confusion about meaning causes more errors than does confusion about sound (Anderson, 1970).

Continuing illustration. In our continuing example, the proficient host-listener was forming mental pictures along with his sound images as he received his guest's message, "Do I see a cot?" Among his encoded meanings was possibly one for "see" (referring to "looking") and one for "cot" (referring to a tan-colored, canvas object with a wooden frame, such as the listener might have had to sleep on when he was a child visiting relatives). Perhaps the listener was even imaging such a cot in the middle of his elegant living room—totally incongruous. Whether by sound or sight, imaging enhances remembering.

Application

By whatever means imaging takes place (sound, sight, touch, taste), reading instructors realize the importance of familiarizing language in the child's ear before expecting the child to "get it in the eye" during reading. Teachers have long known that because children can form a visual thought picture, they can learn to read sight words, such as *airplane,* more easily than such words as *whether, there,* or *was.* The following activities develop applications for auditory picturing.

Image scrimmage. Children can listen with the purpose of forming sensory, auditory images from oral descriptions. After the first presentation of a selection that stimulates especially through its imagery related to sound, the children are asked to analyze how the author could picture them so vividly and then are asked to try to do the same. For example, the children might examine the following phrases for image formation, both visual and auditory: "The ambulance sirening its whining, whirling whoop of sound"; "The snapping, sizzling whine of fireworks on the Fourth of July"; "The whisper of soft grey hairnets of rain"; "Licking his lips, the leopard lolled and lapped his yellow lollipop."

Another activity requires a detailed oral description of, for example, a clown. Then let the children draw what they image and compare it with the original message. Children can check their own imaging ability.

As to spelling, a conscious use of visual imagery is found when a word is pictured as being on a large billboard, each letter fastened there securely with large, fancy nails. This visual image might be accompanied, where appropriate, with an auditory image of the sound associated with the letters. (Primary-intermediate)

Step 5: Search Past Store of Ideas

In the next step listeners may have to search and sort through many possibilities and images stored in their long-term memory. They may also "anticipate" by using this store. They search their past experiences, including their competence in vocabulary, their language background of probabilities, standards or criteria they have formed, ways of organizing, and various purposes and associations. They may need to compare the material with the context of what comes next, if nothing came before. During this step the listener is still using, hopefully, the time difference between the rate of presentation by the speaker and his or her faster speed of thought.

Continuing illustration. The listener in the example might be searching through his associations and possibilities of meaning, comparing and thinking to himself, " 'Cot,' 'cot' . . . could he be referring to 'couch'? But of course there is a couch here. Why would he be asking if he saw one, especially when he is looking over in the other direction into that dark corner?" By comparing the findings of his search, the host is also illustrating the next step.

Step 6: Compare

Having found cues in the message, listeners compare those they selected ("cot") with their previous store of knowledge (which they have just searched). This is done in order to form a tentative image so that they can predict meaning. Here it is possible to see many closely bound steps in proficient listening. The listener may be comparing not only previous knowledge of sound and sentence patterns, but also *larger* organizational or relational structures. The term *larger organizational structure* can refer, for example, to the following: (1) chronological time sequence ("It happened at 5:00, after work."); (2) cause and effect ("because it was rush hour"); (3) part of the whole ("His was one car in a long stream of traffic."); and (5) contrast ("This route now is certainly different from the way it was ten years ago; why, this freeway was a cow path then!") (McCullough, 1968).

Application

To compare, the listener usually needs to use those components called indexing and scanning. For example, a child who lacks indexing and scanning skills fails to flip quickly to the mental file containing *at* clusters when asked to name words that rhyme with *bat* for the class Halloween poem. (I'm not recommending this sort of thing as the most productive activity!) As another example, when a writer searches for the best word, she or he may scan several groups of synonyms to find just the "right" one. Scanning includes partial listening when interest lies only in certain portions of discourse. Children with a scanning problem may be unable to get the general impression of what they hear or be unable to pick out details. For example, when Ted dials the phone for the time of day, he may be inundated by the advertising message, miss the time, and have to call again. Yet he probably could not recall the main idea of the advertising message either. Herbert Spencer once said that when knowledge is not in order, the more of it individuals have, the greater will be their confusion. Indexing and scanning skills help avoid such confusion.

Scanning for organizational cues. Consider using this activity for increasing skill in scanning, searching, and comparing. During practice for scanning for rhetorical cues, listeners should spot hints on: (1) the introduction (when they notice the words, "In overview . . ."); (2) progression or transition (when they spot the words, "The next point . . ."); (3) the conclusion (when they detect the words, "In summary . . ."). Help the children collect signal words and phrases, such as "in the first place," "as a final point," "on the other hand."

After a class discussion of such signal words and phrases, read organized material that uses these cues. Ask pupils to tell or record when they recognize a turning point or some other signal that shows a relationship among ideas. Pupils can devise selections for partners to scan as they listen. The following are some examples: additions *(also, besides);* time *(at last, meanwhile);* explanation *(for example, in other words, on the far side);* comparison *(similarly);* contrast *(however, but);* and cause and effect *(because, on account of).* (Intermediate-middle school)

Step 7: Test the Cues

Listeners have now compared the signals from the speaker with their repertory of possibilities. Next, if listeners cannot readily make a choice regarding an idea (hypothesis) about the message, they may ask the speaker to help them. This provides assistance in *testing* their cues or in selecting them. Listeners may do this by asking a question or by attempting a summary of what they think the speaker said. If possible, listeners should compare a larger context of sound sequences with their internal store of information. When listeners test their cues about their hypothesis and get a "match," they can then progress to understanding meaning and its use. If they fail to get a "match," back they go for further search and the next most likely idea, unless they just quit.

Continuing illustration. In the continuing example, our host-listener might test the cues by questioning his guest aloud: "What did you say, a 'cot,' something one sleeps on?"

In essence, the host-listener's testing of hypotheses functioned like this: upon hearing and processing this message, he got a likely identification, which he tested to see how well it fit the cues of context, common sense, and (now, if possible) feedback from the speaker. The proficient listener operates in large part by sampling activity focused on hypothesis testing.

Application

Children show individual and developmental differences in sampling skill and in testing cues. Few need the whole word to make a correct identification. If you should hear the sounds represented by "Now he lis . . .," you probably would guess correctly from the sample and the context that "listens" would be the last word. You work with the probabilities of your language and children do too. As they grow older they increase their ability to judge from samples and to test cues.

Experienced listeners, who process only 50 percent of the sounds in their environment, piece out from parts, "tuning out" the rest, listening with "half an ear." While sampling and testing, proficient listeners try to select the fewest possible cues to make the best possible choice (Ammon, 1969). However, individual differences are likely to occur. While Jim might be an accurate "word-by-word" listener, he might not be so skillful at thoughtful analysis of extended conversations. Taking "bite" sizes that are too small, he gets lost in detail when he tries to use his listening to solve a complex problem for which he needs a broad perspective.

A final aspect of cue testing with possible classroom applications is called *monitoring.* Listeners check to see if they have heard what they thought they heard. During monitoring, children may catch mistakes in their own speech when the sounds they just made are processed. For example, in a conversation they might say: "He don't know—er—He *doesn't* know." A great deal of learning by listening takes place through going back for testing and correction. The same is true of regression in reading. This is an aspect overlooked and undervalued by some reading instructors. Again, the speculation about letting children think and talk out loud to themselves about their lessons fits in here.

Testing with context clues. To develop this step consider activities that employ and test a variety of context clues developed by experience, definition, synonym, comparison, or summary. In the following examples the category is given with its illustration. The word to be gotten from context is underlined. Further explanation is given in some cases.

Experience: "The man was hit on the head, punched in the nose, and had his wallet stolen. He met with <u>foul play</u>." Note how the earlier context gives the clues (that might be categorized as experience) for the meaning of the words <u>foul play,</u> should the child not know what these words mean.

Definition: "The tube contained the fluid part of the blood, the <u>plasma</u>." Note how the earlier part of the sentence serves as a set of cues to help a child in testing out the meaning of the word *plasma,* should the child not already know its meaning.

Synonym: "She received the formal letter, the <u>epistle</u>."

Comparison: "One boat stayed right side up, but the other <u>capsized</u>."

Summary: "They all appeared uncivilized, rude, wild, and showy in their dress and manner. In essence, they were <u>barbaric</u>."

Have the children check their comparisons by testing the cues and their hypotheses against you or against a dictionary. (Intermediate-middle school)

Step 8: Recode

Probably one of the first reactions persons have to words they notice in a message is to say them to themselves. They recode spoken symbols by noting changes in sound and in the order in which they occur. As they regroup the sounds, they may translate them into images while they rehearse the sounds to themselves. Or the listener may simply be able to go directly to meaning with little recoding (see Liberman, Mattingly, and Turvey, 1972).

Continuing illustration. Our host-listener might be saying to himself, "Cot? Sot? Toc? What in the world does he mean?" He proceeds from the raw sound to try for a match with the language codes he knows. He uses all of the rules, strategies, and reorganizations he thinks might fit. In this case, recoding is a key problem. Although the host is trying, he has failed to find the appropriate recoding.

A listener may go from code to code. For example, she or he may find it necessary to recode by translating Swedish into Danish if Danish is better known to the listener, and then into English. In the last chapter it was mentioned that dialects, such as black English, may be recoded into other dialects and pronunciations. But all of this recoding during the listening act may or may not lead to comprehension of meaning. Similarly, in reading it is possible to recode from letter to sound and still fail to have any grasp of what the author's message is all about.

Application

Recoding is common not only in movement among dialects, but also in processing ordinary oral language. Besides the recoding of dialect, reorganization of language sound and structures is discernible, for instance, in almost any spontaneous tape recording. When there is an opportunity to play back a sample of informal conversation or to read a transcript from which nothing has been omitted, most of us are surprised (appalled?) at our language. As we change our minds in midstream, there usually will be clutter, repetition or redundancy, unfinished ideas, unintentional sound substitutions, garbled mazes, even apparent slips of grammar or usage from our native dialect. There will also tend to be some general incoherence. Such examples are found on TV talk shows, in interviews, and even in presidential speeches. Aided by redundancies, listeners do much recoding in pursuit of meaning. If teachers and parents realize this kind of error is normal, they can be more patient with children, especially those who speak varying dialects. The following activities indicate further applications of this step.

Recoding dialects. One of the games grows out of listening to recordings of various dialects and engaging in recoding. You might use, for example, the Folkways recording (a 12-inch LP) "Instructional Record for Regional Speech Patterns" or the dialect side of the McGraw-Hill recording "Our Changing Language." You might read from conversations in dialect in children's books, such as *Tom Sawyer,* Natalie Carlson's *The Empty Schoolhouse,* or Wilt James's *Smoky.* Or you might tape-record your own material. See if the children can recode back into their own dialect, then back again into the original language. See if they can put a common phrase into various dialects.

Slurvien language. Devise and try out in the classroom some of your own contributions to the "Slurvien language" to illustrate the proficient listener's act of recoding.[8] Slurvien sentences are composed of actual words or names in our language. When these are slurred sufficiently or spread apart when spoken, they can be "symbolized" by other words. At first glance (or first hearing) the words seem to be nonsense. But a skillful listener can recode the slurred words into an old familiar line or saying. Correspondence is not complete, but elements are close enough when slurred to make the recoding leap possible.

Consider this line: "Rocker buy bay be inner treat hop." Say this line aloud quickly several times to see if you can recode it into a familiar line. Better yet, get someone else to say it, slurring the words together quickly. If you are able to recode it to a familiar line, several factors emerge. Even if they are not well articulated, bursts of sound separated by pauses are translatable because of pattern, major vowels, and stress. A successful recoding shows that people give little attention, actually, to individual sounds of a language written in an arbitrary manner. Since we receive in rapid speech much auditory information that comes quickly, we are fortunate to have redundancy and the three elements as language markers. Of twenty individual speech sounds, approximately two-thirds may give us enough information to grasp the message. In translating Slurvien listeners find themselves moving beyond analysis and synthesis of the information as they seemingly put their brains into neutral and coast. Then, "Ah ha!"—they have it. By now you have probably recoded the Slurvien example "Rocker buy bay be inner treat hop" into "Rock-a-bye baby in a tree top."

Next, look at this example of Slurvien: "Turnip out fir ply." Say it rapidly over and over. Among other variations in articulation the recoder substitutes *p* for *b* (a common exchange for the interpreter of slurred speech) as he or she turns "Turnip out fir ply" into "Turn about's fair play."

Some people have great difficulty with this task. For example, they are unable to translate "Kep pass tiff up hurl hip" into "Keep a stiff upper lip," even when they are familiar with the saying. People schooled in the application of the International Phonetic Alphabet (IPA)[9] will usually have an edge in the game of unraveling Slurvien.

One of the skills of the proficient listener is this ability to recode by sampling information and relying on pattern, major vowels, and stress. Of course, it also helps to have the original saying established firmly in the language background. Also, it helps to realize that the task is to translate the saying into an old familiar line, such as "Oswell attend swell" into "All's well that ends well." Older elementary school children can have fun devising these Slurvien phrases at the same time that they sharpen their awareness of certain language features. To review, these features are pattern, major vowels, stress, pause, the arbitrary nature of written language, and the importance of being orally familiar with the language.

Highly Conscious Intellectual Activity

Beyond that part of the definition labeled Attention finally emerges the part labeled Intellectual Activity. It may represent a highly conscious culmination. The first four parts were labeled: Previous Knowledge, Material, Physiological Activity, and Attention. In the fifth part of the definition, the two remaining major divisions of listener activity (Getting Meaning and Thinking Beyond Listening) and their steps conclude this definition (review Figure 4).

Getting Meaning

The first major division of highly conscious, intellectual listener activity, getting meaning, could be broken down into many steps reflecting a variety of skills. The step chosen to illustrate this division, however, consists mainly of literal interpretation in terms of simple, accurate, tested relationships.[10]

Step 9: Get Meaning (Literal Comprehension)

After listeners have noted sound, formed images, recoded, and tested hypotheses, they may think about relationships in order to decide what the message means to them. For example, the listener may link sounds heard with verbs (the man *tossed* the grenade) or with prepositions (*beyond* the crowd). They may do this as an aid to retention, association, and comprehension. (As used here, "decode" is a synonym for obtaining literal understanding from the oral message.)

Continuing illustration. To return to the example, suppose the foreign-born guest helps the listener-host by a bit of gesturing, thereby indicating whiskers and claws. The listener then uses these nonverbal cues to help him recode accurately and get the meaning. The listener says, "Oh, oh, 'cat' is what you said, not 'cot'! Why yes, I didn't know that she was in here. Yes; it's a Siamese."

Indicating that he has achieved meaning, the listener-host may be saying something such as this to himself: "At *last* I figured out that one! He asked if he saw my *cat,* not a *cot.*" The meaning intended for the term "listening" is realized when the receiver reaches the point in this series of steps where his experience brings meaning to the verbal symbols. The listener-host is now in a position to make appropriate responses to the speaker.

Application

As illustrated earlier, the meaning that the listener decides upon at one time may or may not be the same as the intended meaning of the speaker. As was mentioned in the last chapter, meaning is seldom found in a single word or phrase. The broader relationships of "who" says "what" to "whom" and "under what circumstances" give meaning to a language unit.

To carry this idea further, according to the view of general semantics, it follows that meaning is not in the word but in the person who is using it. It is the transfer of meaning that is the goal of listening. Since meaning is in the user, meanings change. They change according to the identity of the communicators (students, teachers, friends, enemies), varying contexts (Alabama, Appalachia, campuses, factories, fiestas), and time (morning, night, tomorrow, five years later, twenty years earlier).

Since common words have no inherent meanings, the teacher can encourage children to ask questions designed to transfer comprehension. Such questions are "What?" "Where?" "What time?" and "What do *you* mean?" (not "What does *it* mean?"). Encourage children to search for experiences that are common to both sender and receiver, because a word is rarely, if ever, identical to the event it reports. As general semanticists would say, the word is not the thing. The following activity further develops some of these ideas.

Which meaning? As an activity used to check for comprehension of *multiple meanings,* children can listen to pairs of sentences that have specific words used with two different meanings. For the first pair, write so that the children can see as well as hear the messages and get the idea of the game. Then let them listen only. Children are to find in the first sentence a word that can be used in the second sentence. Then they tell (or picture) what each of the two uses of the word means to them. Here are two examples; children can construct others. (Primary-intermediate)

> If you *lean* against that glass, it might break.
> I want a piece of _____ steak.

> He used a *switch* to make the mule go.
> Why don't you _____ to another TV station?

For some common words *(clear, cross, run)* children may find in the dictionary column after column of multiple definitional material, a confusing mass of fine print. While you probably use only about 2,000 words in talking to your listeners each day, the 5,000 words you use over-all probably have about 14,000 definitions in the dictionary. That number seems meager, however, when every moment of life brings experiences unlike any experience you had before. Although a dictionary may give various meanings for different contexts, it fails to tell what a word "means." *Meaning is found in user context.*

Thinking Beyond Listening

Once listeners have accurately received a message, they can go on to productive thought and response far beyond the event. They may employ the perceived meaning in further intellectual activity. For example, they might go on to respond with such purposes as the following: classifying parts of a message (according to time, space, position, degree, etc.); ranking information (according to its importance and relevance); making comparisons; defining; assigning sequence; predicting; applying; seeing cause-effect relationships; planning procedures; evaluating critically; and appreciating the drama, tone, rhythm, and lyric quality ("turning on"). I have often suggested that the listener might unify and interrelate all of this mental activity through creative problem solving (Lundsteen, 1976a, 1976b).

Step 10: Intellectualize (Beyond Listening)

In this last step the listener thinks beyond listening. One reason for its importance is that it facilitates learning if it includes processing that is deep, full, meaningful, and filled with purpose.

Purposes of listening, which may be similar to those for reading, have a wide range. The objectives range all the way from playing with simple sounds to literal comprehension, sophisticated interpretation, and intense emotional experience. The following are examples:

> The apparent purpose may be merely *passive.*[11] ("Hum-m-m, that person has a nice-sounding voice.")
>
> The purpose may be to use the mind in *associating* or in

classifying. ("Someone who would use a word such as that does not belong to my generation.")

It may be listening in order to *organize* or to *synthesize.* ("I think he is trying to define *peace;* it could be organized into a definition with a little reworking.")

It may be using the mind to listen *critically,* according to some highly conscious standard. ("What does he know about peace? It doesn't seem to begin with him!")

The listener may have an *emotional, appreciative* purpose in mind. ("Ah-h-h, what a poetic choice of words; if only I could speak as well as that.")

Or the purpose may be to engage in *problem solving* while listening. ("That suggestion for a survey could be one of the first steps in our attack on noise pollution.")

Continuing illustration. Finally, the listener-host might think beyond listening, even with such a small slice of discourse. His thoughts might run in this fashion: "Oh, O.K. My guest pronounces 'cat' like 'cot.' I wonder what other languages would sound 'cat' as 'cot.' 'Cot,' 'cot,' I like that accent. Maybe I should offer to help him with his English and he could help me with my Italian."

Application

The following are a few classroom activities that can be used to promote this step.

Black-white. In this simple listening and thinking game, you and your children can explore meaning and interpretation further. Use small groups with complementary abilities. The leader speaks a word and asks a player to speak a word that means the opposite. The children can keep a record of their successes. For the primary grades use, at first, simple words with obvious opposites: light-dark, stop-go, up-down, young-old, North Pole-South Pole, work-play. Then the children might talk about how opposites may shade into one another, depending upon the point of view; for example "work" to one person may be "play" to another. (An example is the whitewashing of the fence in *Tom Sawyer.*) (Primary-intermediate-middle school)

Hitchhike story. Someone in the group starts a tale, e.g., "It was a blustery, gale-blown night . . ." At a given signal the teller halts and another listener must pick up and continue to weave the story. Proceed in this fashion through the group. (Primary-intermediate)

The Step Framework in Retrospect

The summary diagram of the ten steps of proficient listening (Figure 5) is by no means technically precise. Occurrences may proceed in more of a hop, skip, and jump fashion, and the steps are not entirely independent of one another.[12] Most statements based on this framework are tenuous; they are made solely to provide a basis for definition and later objectives. Knowledge of the listening process, listening characteristics of children, and teaching strategies, their effects, and their development are still primitive (Carroll, 1968; Devine, 1978). But now that educators are learning more about listening—the advantages, educability, and deficits—listening as a crucial language art is unlikely to "go away."

To meet growing needs, the following flow chart of steps can serve as a springboard for planning of both curriculum and instruction. Use of this framework brings the listening process to higher consciousness and facilitates reaching problem areas. A helpful curriculum may need, at some time or other, to take all of these steps into account. *The point is that listening is complex and that many listening skills have been largely passed over in the curriculum.* A framework of steps brings these skills to a necessary level of awareness. As you learn more and more about the listeners in your classroom, it is suggested that you manipulate this framework of steps, add to it, alter it, and make it your own. See how much of it you can integrate into challenging, creative, problem-oriented activities. Use it as an organizing framework on which to hang isolated activities, games, and bits of information as you accumulate them. Then you can retrieve, arrange, and justify them in a more interrelated way.

The three major divisions of listener activity are summarized in Figure 5, which draws upon work by Goodman in Gephart (1970). You may have thought of several items that appear to be missing from this framework of steps. For example, there are probably different stages of listening development (prenatal to old age) relating to each of the three facets: the material, the background, and the skills (see Weaver and Rutherford, 1974; Rossiter, 1970). As the listener develops skills over a long period of time, beginning with the ability to hear in intrauterine life, these facets probably

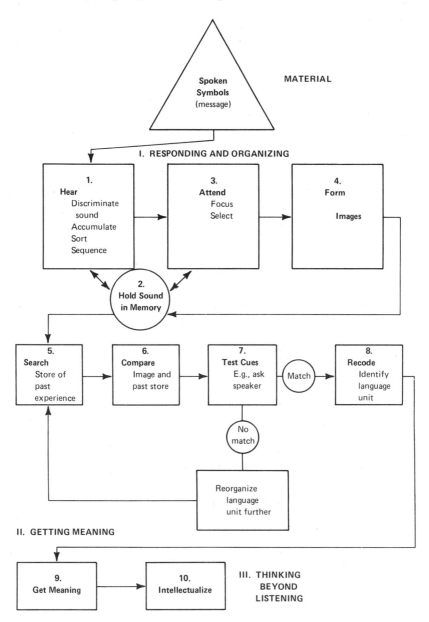

Fig. 5. Flowchart of the steps a proficient listener may take.

act on one another in differing ways. Also missing from this
listener framework are all of the filters and distortions of masking,
from noise and fatigue to personal blocks and destructive habits.
They are missing partly because this is a chart for a proficient
listener who knows how to cope efficiently with these blocks.
Also omitted are elements of self-centered (egocentric) communication (Flavel, 1968; Lundsteen, 1976a, pp. 436-7; also see
chapter three).

A caution: when researchers suggest a performance hierarchy,
some teachers may appropriate it unwisely and use it as a rigid
accountability model. However, listening, as is reading, is more
than a sum of isolated skills. The idea of fitting skill upon skill, as
in constructing a tinker toy (popular in accountability models of
teaching), will not solve most problems. "Tinker-toy" teaching
alone is unlikely to turn children into proficient communicators.
Much about being a proficient listener is still unknown, an in-
explicable recombination and synthesis of behaviors, attitudes,
and feelings that are more than the separate parts. Keeping this
caution in mind, the teacher's ability to know and skillfully
analyze parts of listening and account for some of them may help
at least some children to an extent never achieved before.

Conclusion

The definition at the opening of this chapter was: "Listening
refers to the process by which spoken language is converted to
meaning in the mind." The components have been clarified as
follows: *listening* as distinguished from physiological hearing and
from attention; *process* as made up of steps; *spoken language* as
having various dimensions in material; *meaning* as residing in the
users (with need for testing cues and for feedback); and *mind* as
capable of intellectualizing far beyond the received message.
Additionally, if we listen well, we make an appropriate response
to what the speaker says to us. But keep in mind that complex
processes are inadequately defined in one sentence or even in
one paragraph.

Additional Activities

The major step in the listening process to which each of the
following activities applies is given in parentheses after the activity
along with grade level. As you discover and use other listening

activities in the classroom, consider the specific knowledge to be gained by observing the children.

Mime it. In this activity memory and sequence play a part. After the manner of "follow the leader," the first player (standing and without a chair) mimes and describes his or her action (e.g., "I am throwing a Frisbee"). Moving in a clockwise direction, the next player repeats that action and adds one of his or her own ("I am throwing a Frisbee and holding a kite"), and so on until someone forgets some of the preceding additions. Children can leave their chairs, arranged in a circle with one less chair than the number of children, and follow the leader around the inside of the circle, miming as they walk, adding players, and adding to the repeated sequence. When someone misses, everyone must scramble for the empty chairs. The player left standing starts the next round of remembered mimes. (Step 2. Primary-intermediate-middle school)

Dream it. Have a group of children suggest a number of items they can dream about: a puppy, candy, a merry-go-round, a fire. Have the leader hold up a card with the letter of the alphabet that matches the beginning letter of one of the topics suggested, such as an *M*. Children who recall the *M* word as "merry-go-round" can pantomime the word, sketch it, write it, or say it. The memory factor can be made easier or more difficult by the nature and number of the words to be kept in mind. Again, keep records for diagnostic purposes. For older children associational and organizational ploys to aid memory could be discussed, for example, remembering a larger number of items by associating each with a room of a house. A vivid sensory imaging might also be tried. (Step 2. Primary-intermediate)

Gossip. The old game of gossip uses a whispered message passed from person to person and finally spoken aloud by the last person to receive it; the original message is then stated by the first person. This activity illustrates many aspects of hearing and listening, including auditory discrimination and analysis. (Step 1. Primary-intermediate)

Word ping-pong. Pairs of children are given a list of words. At a signal, one child speaks a word and her or his partner must say a word that rhymes with it. The two continue back and forth until one child cannot think of another rhyming word and forfeits a point to the other player, or until there is a general signal to start with another word. Or the point can be forfeited after the lapse of an agreed upon length of time. Once you determine which children are skilled in discriminating rhyming, they can assist, for brief periods, those children who are less skilled. (Step 1. Primary-intermediate-middle school)

Catch it? Give a short prepared talk or tell a story and have children listen for all the *uh*'s you use, sounds you substitute, numbers you mention, sounds you mention, and so on. If the children are assigned the roles of characters or objects in the story, each time a character or object is mentioned, the player is to jump up and make a sound or a motion characteristic of the assigned role. (Step 3. Primary-intermediate)

Musical cutouts. A variation on musical chairs is to tape large cutouts to the floor at various points around a circle (planets, animals, geometric shapes, states). Players march, skip, etc., around the circle, stepping on each cutout as they come to it. When the music, reading, or sound stops, any player whose foot is not on a cutout is eliminated for one or more rounds. The players might also be asked to identify his or her cutout or give a word that begins with the same sound or that rhymes with it. (Step 3. Primary-intermediate)

Attending to reverses. The leader, walking around, suddenly touches a part of his or her clothing, body, or belongings and deliberately misidentifies it (or correctly identifies it). For example, he or she might say, "This is my shoe," and touch his or her shirt instead (or do it correctly). The leader then points to one of the players, who gives a reverse response if the leader has mis-identified, "This is my shirt," and then touches a shoe. If several small groups are playing this game at the same time, children will be getting practice in attending during competing messages. (Steps 3-10. Primary-intermediate)

Reflecting on a poem. Select two poems, one to read just for enjoyment without comment and one to promote conscious thinking aloud after listening. The following stanzas from a poem by Sara Brandon Rickey have provoked thought and discussion in classrooms:

Water Magic

A rainbow comes, a rainbow goes
In rhythm with my sprinkling hose.
It arches over my green lawn
In colors seen at early dawn,

And then it disappears; but where?
How does it hide itself in air?
How does it reappear again,
Forming itself from hose or rain?

Children might be enticed to express their feelings about the rhythmic, lyrical quality. They might be encouraged to recall their own comparisons. Children may reconstruct the experience of looking into a sheet of water droplets (rain, fog, spray) that is illuminated by strong, white light from behind them. They may recall seeing one, sometimes two rainbows, the inner one brighter, narrower, with colors reversed (red on the outside, violet on the inside edge of the smaller one). They might clarify the kind of sprinkling hose that the poet was probably talking about. As they examine their wonderings about cause-effect relationships between the spray, the light, and the colors, they might plan procedures for finding information and for making their own rainbows to talk and write about. (All steps)

Noise pollution solution. After, for example, a walk down the street, the teacher could suggest the following activities: list all of the noises heard; list, or tell, three words or phrases that describe the noises; decide whether the noises were pleasant or unpleasant; if there were too many highly unpleasant noises, plan steps to overcome each of them. (Steps 3-10)

3 Towards a Listening Taxonomy

The first chapter placed listening in the context of the other language arts; the second chapter gave a detailed view of the various parts and steps contributing to proficient listening. The final part of this framework included getting meaning and thinking beyond listening—both of which are aspects of comprehension. This chapter elaborates ideas about skills, especially for listening comprehension—the major concern of most classroom teachers. Most sections of this chapter are based on questions, indicated by quotes, that teachers have asked, for example, "Can I find a specific sequence of listening skills that children need?" In other words, what are some of the instructional objectives? Understanding how skills are generated gives teachers a feeling of confidence in a time of pressures for accountability and a better basis for decision making and evaluation of programs.

Why All of This Attention to Skills?

Currently there is an unfortunately increasing attitude that "If you can't test it, it isn't there or it isn't important." Consequently, it appears wise to concentrate creative efforts on assessing the crucial higher levels of comprehension-thinking skills stimulated by listening; otherwise, they are lost. However, at the same time that pressure is being exerted for testing specific skills, some performance contractors are discovering that currently used achievement tests are totally ineffective. These tests rank children to the nth degree of precision around a "meaningless average that fails to reflect genuinely appropriate goals of instruction" (Markel, 1973).

If the evils inherent in poor tests and the pressures for measuring trivia are kept in mind, effective instruction will be based on clearly defined skills and behaviors. Consider the instructor who plans in this manner: "I am going to set up an activity and a method of observing that will show me if this child is distinguishing fact from opinion in this type of sentence, using this type of question, calling for this type of response." This instructor, who is aware of the benefits of careful planning, will probably have pupils who are achieving listening skill more rapidly than those of the teacher who says vaguely, "I'm going to teach more listening." If the first teacher also has a probable sequence of listening development in mind (rather than considering listening as an isolated activity), greater gains for the child are more likely to result. And if this teacher also attends to the attitudes being created and realizes that listening instruction pays off during creative problem solving, gains will probably be far more genuine and long lasting. To put it another way, the hope is that teachers will at least go beyond the type of skill objective that reads: "After listening to what I have to say, the child will be able to tell me what I said" (Markle, 1973). The ideal is for educators to help the greatest possible number of children to achieve both cognitive and affective goals at the highest levels. But it is indeed hard to be precise as to just what goals and objectives to use. Thus, a typical question from teachers—"What listening skills do children need most?"

What Is a Useful Progression of Listening Skills?

Presently, educators are unable to say, "Here is *the* list of listening skills." In fact, when one investigator went about asking teachers, "What *is* a listening skill?" he found that virtually no one knew of any at all (Kellogg, 1966).[1] Consider the following method of generating those skills called the A, B, C's of listening.

The three letters represent three levels ranging from the least to the most intellectually complex. Level A represents the lowest level of skills in *acuity* (or perception of sound). Level B represents *basic discrimination* among sounds.[2] The most intellectually complex, Level C, represents *comprehension* of what the sounds mean. At Level C, sounds become meaningful words and discourse (linguistically symbolic). Skills at Levels A, B, and C may thus form a hierarchy because persons who fail to discriminate sound differences with finesse probably also fail to symbolize much verbal meaning from those sounds. If they cannot recognize meaning, they cannot think or talk about it.

Once skills for the three levels are pinpointed, the next job is to superimpose types or sounds upon these A, B, C's of listening. The sounds are those made in nature, those made by artificial objects, and those made in speaking. Some children need to begin a listening program by learning to give discriminating attention to sounds in nature and from artificial objects in order to establish a pleasant tone and to develop patterns of success.

If a teacher combines the two levels of skill and sound, he or she can develop a grid for generating objectives (such as that in Figure 6). The darkened cell in the bottom righthand corner (Language Comprehension) warrants some further explanation.

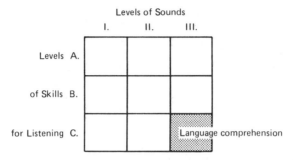

Fig. 6. By combining the A, B, C's of listening—acuity, basic discrimination, and comprehension—with types of sound—those made in nature, those made by artificial objects, and those made in speaking—teachers can develop a grid for identifying listening program objectives.

What Are the Skills Levels in Language Comprehension?

Language comprehension represents an area of much concern to educators. The teacher can use just this behavior "cell" and expand its framework by running various skills of comprehension down one side of a related matrix and various units of language across another. Units of language might begin with words or even with sounds within words. Then might follow sentences (or grammar). These units might be followed by paragraphs and then by the total composition. This last complete unit of discourse, during which many relations and organizations emerge, is frequently neglected in listening instruction and is indispensable to the adequate teaching of comprehension.

Next, the skills of comprehension should be elaborated. The discussion here reflects a traditional classification described in B. S. Bloom's *Taxonomy of Educational Objectives* (1956). Briefly, the progressive dimensions of Bloom's taxonomy include the following:

1. Knowledge of specifics. Recall and recognition: Who? What? Where? When? Too often teachers stop here when seeking responses and never encourage pupils to respond at the higher levels.

2. Comprehension. Translation (How else can it be said?), interpretation (What does it mean? How does it relate?), extrapolation (What came before? What is next?).

3. Application. How do you use it? How do you use it in still another way?

4. Analysis. What are its parts? How do you classify them?

5. Creative synthesis. Includes divergent thinking and creative problem solving: how do you form new "wholes," invent, and compose, using your own ideas?

6. Evaluation. Judge, using standards; choose, tell why; debate means and ends.

Figure 7 elaborates these steps in language comprehension.[3] Examples of skills based on this chart might be: listening to recall a detail mentioned in a paragraph, e.g., number of miles (possible classification: Knowledge of Specifics—Paragraph; see X_1 marking the skill in the matrix of Figure 7); and listening to learn how one idea or part of a play (the theme) has been related to an idea within it, e.g., a character's behavior (possible classification: Analysis—Total Composition; see X_2 in righthand column of Figure 7). If a teacher follows the grid, skills for development that move from simple to more complex and from smaller language units to larger can be selected.

Comprehension Skills	Units of Language Organization			
	Word	Sentence	Paragraph	Total Composition
General Listening Knowledge of specifics			X_1	
Comprehension				
Application				
Analysis				X_2
Synthesis				
Critical Listening Evaluation				

Fig. 7. A grid for classifying listening comprehension skills.

Units of Language Organization				
Phonology	Lexicon		Grammar	
(sound)	Morphemes, Words, Idioms	Semantic and Grammatical Components of Lexicon	Morphology and Syntax	Semantic Components

Fig. 8. A language unit classification scheme suggested by the work of Carroll (1968).

An alternate to Kellogg's simple recommendation for language units is a classification suggested from the work of Carroll (1968). This scheme could be added at the top of Figure 8. Thus, a more detailed classification of language-signaling systems and information processing might include not only the semantic meaning of words, sentences, paragraphs, and compositions but also at least (1) the ways word affixes influence their semantic meaning and syntactic function; (2) the ways phrases and deep structures are assigned to sentences; (3) the ways surface and deep structures of sentences govern the modifications of word and phrase meaning; (4) the identification of antecedents of pronouns, pro-verbs, and words or phrases standing for another phrase, sentence, or larger unit in a passage (anaphora); and (5) the ways structures are assigned to and modify that which in spoken discourse might constitute paragraphs and larger units of discourse (Bormuth, 1969). This classification does not mean, "Teach children formal grammar and rhetoric." Children can learn to respond to the signaling systems of language without having conscious knowledge of even the existence of formal grammar and rhetoric (Bormuth, 1969). It does mean that developers should take language units into account when formulating skills (see Figure 9 for the relationship).

The next example illustrates how all six of these levels of comprehension can be called for in the total composition known as advertising. Each of the various objectives might be placed on task cards in a learning center file. A child could start with the first and easiest questions on the level of knowledge of specifics and move on to questions that require higher and higher levels of comprehension skill.[4]

Comprehension Skills	Units of Language Organization			
	Word	Sentence	Paragraph	Total Composition
General listening				
Synthesis				
Analysis				
Application				
Comprehension				
Knowledge of specifics				
Critical listening Evaluation				

Fig. 9. A scheme for listening skills development that takes into account the language units shown in Figure 8.

Task Cards for Developing Levels of Comprehension

Strand: Listening to Media—Advertising and Television

Overall Objective: The child will analyze, compose, and evaluate an original TV advertisement.

Social Studies Concept: *Demand* is consumer willingness to buy a certain product at a given price.

1. Knowledge of specifics: Become an ad collector. Use food advertisements for examples or use a tape recorder to "collect" or recall commercials for different brands of a product you have chosen. Note the differences in the ads.

2. Comprehension: Using your own words, summarize and rewrite the commercials, aiming for an audience of your own age group or another selected group.

3. Application: Make a survey, asking (1) What is the person's favorite commercial about the product? (2) Why is it appealing to him or her? (3) Does it influence him or her to buy the product? Apply what you have understood and the skills you have developed from making earlier surveys.

4. Analysis: What are the minimum elements of an advertisement if it is to present necessary information? What are its parts? Conduct a survey to determine from a sample of "consumers" those parts of the advertisements that affect them most and why. Try to include different types of consumers in your

survey. If the advertisement is for food, spot how much nutritional information is actually given. Analyze how your reactions about the food (based on persuasion through child actors, lights, words, and canned laughter) might affect your health.

5. Synthesis: Write and produce your own thirty-second commercial for a product. Decide what audience you are appealing to and how you will appeal.

6. Evaluation: Plan and carry out an evaluation of your advertisement. Ask a sample of potential consumers to react to your ad. Were you successful in light of the criteria you had set? Why or why not? What are the essential parts of this kind of composing if a demand is to be created? What moral or ethical ideas (rights and wrongs) do you need to consider about the impact of the ad on viewers, such as their nutrition and health?

If this set of questions was placed in a task file box in a learning center in a classroom, it might be only one of several.[5] Other related questions could be designed to help a child attain a certain social studies (or other content area) concept at the same time that he or she was practicing specific listening comprehension skills. Of course, when listeners are engaged in creative problem solving through listening, they are meaningfully using and interrelating all of the various levels of skills.

If six levels of comprehension seem too complex, then consider grouping them into just two levels labeled "general listening" and "critical listening" (to the left of the chart, Figure 7). The term *critical* implies the use of highly conscious standards or criteria for evaluating spoken material after it has been comprehended. This classification would split the Bloom taxonomy in two, with the first five levels in the first group and the last level, "evaluation," by itself. *Evaluation*, synonymous with *critical*, is supposedly the most difficult or complex comprehension process. Evaluation encompasses all of the earlier levels of the Bloom taxonomy. The following is a typical collection of such skills or goals:

General Listening

1. Remembering significant details accurately (knowledge of specifics)
2. Remembering simple sequences of words and ideas
3. Following oral directions
4. Paraphrasing a spoken message (comprehension by translation)

5. Following a sequence in (a) plot development, (b) character development, (c) speaker's argument

6. Understanding denotative (literal) meanings of words

7. Understanding connotative meanings of words (comprehension by interpretation)

8. Understanding meanings of words from spoken context (comprehension by translation and interpretation)

9. Listening for implications of significant details (analysis and interpretation)

10. Listening for implications of main ideas

11. Answering and formulating questions (interactive listening)

12. Identifying main ideas and summarizing (combining and synthesizing the who, what, when, where, and why)

13. Understanding relationships among ideas and the organizational pattern well enough to predict what may come next (comprehension by extrapolation)

14. Connecting the spoken material with previous experience and planning action (application)

15. Listening to imagine and to extend for enjoyment and emotional response (affective-toned synthesizing)

Skill 15 might include appreciation of the aesthetic and dialectical richness, felicity of phrasing, rhythmic flow, sensed emotions, moods, and manner of delivery. The listener demonstrating this skill might appreciate the inquisitive scrape of an opening drawer, the gossipy whisper of a broom.

It might be a mistake to say that there is no highly conscious standard applied to evaluative thinking when this first group of general listening skills is used. But evaluative thinking is present to a far higher and more conscious degree in the skills of critical listening:[6]

Critical Listening

1. Distinguishing fact from fancy, according to criteria

2. Judging validity and adequacy of main ideas, arguments, and hypotheses

3. Distinguishing well-supported statements from opinion and judgment and evaluating them

4. Distinguishing well-supported statements from irrelevant ones and evaluating them

5. Inspecting, comparing, and contrasting ideas and arriving at a conclusion about statements, such as the appropriateness and appeal of one descriptive word over another

6. Evaluating the use of fallacies, such as: (a) self-contradictions, (b) avoiding the question at issue, (c) hasty or false generalization, (d) false analogy, (e) failure to present all choices, (f) appealing to ignorance

7. Recognizing and judging the effects of various devices the speaker may use to influence the listener, such as (a) music, (b) "loaded" words, (c) voice intonation, (d) play on emotional and controversial issues, (e) propaganda, sales pressure—that is, identifying affective loading in communication and evaluating it

8. Detecting and evaluating the bias and prejudice of a speaker or of a point of view

9. Evaluating the qualifications of a speaker

10. Planning to evaluate the ways in which a speaker's ideas might be applied in a new situation[7]

Once listening (and reading) goes beyond physical reception, the skill includes the intellectual thought processes, including the ability to make intellectual distinctions and to reason. These are the mental processes, whether the intake comes from oral language or from print. *However, a natural progression of instruction would be to teach thinking skills in an oral context before expecting thinking skills to serve children to their best advantage in reading and in writing.* Work on advanced comprehension skills should begin during listening.

Successful teaching of any of these higher level skills may call for steps in concept attainment (Lundsteen, 1976a, pp. 46-50). Briefly, concept attainment calls for guiding generalizations to be drawn from examples and nonexamples, encouraging pupils to give examples, and testing with additional examples. (The reader will find creative problem-solving tasks related to higher levels of listening comprehension at the end of this chapter.)

Can Comprehension Skills Be Defined More Rigorously?

Comprehension has so far been defined almost entirely in terms of mental processes. But since these processes are not directly observable, attempts to describe them in terms of skills are confusing to practically everyone. These skills are probably invented in this way: authors begin by trying to examine their own mental activities as they listen (or read); as they examine them, they try to identify each of the different processes they employ. After they identify each of their mental processes, they try to describe them; next they may devise a test to measure each skill. Finally, they sometimes submit their tests to a panel of judges. Teachers are told, for example, that one important listening skill is comprehension of facts. That sounds easy to handle, but the definitions of this skill never explain what a "fact" might be or how to decide if it is "important."[8]

Listening comprehension becomes less tangled when it refers precisely to an increase in the amount of information a child can exhibit as a result of exposure to the specifics of language. We must remember that a child's comprehension is a complex response to the following linguistic specifics: a language system; rules describing how the system transmits information; and specific features of language emerging from devices in rhetoric, semantics, logic, and structural linguistics. Thus, four clarifying criteria for skills (see also Carroll, 1968) are as follows:

> Does the task relate to a definite language feature? E.g., *John* told Bill to go. Who told Bill to go? (Recall of relative pronoun antecedent.)
>
> Does the task, including the question asked, enable the child to use the skill that the teacher thinks it does? For example, if a child hears that a "logomowheel" fits into a "gasket," she or he can answer the question about where a logomowheel fits without any comprehension of what it is. Must the child listen to the test passage to answer, or does unconscious knowledge of sentence structure, or common sense, suggest the correct answer?
>
> Is the construction of the task as concretely objective as possible? For example, the task "Write a paper showing that you grasp the significance of listening" is not very objective. "List four listening comprehension skills in order of complexity and based on the Bloom taxonomy" is more objective.
>
> Can a teacher set many similar tasks in order to elicit a precise definition?[9]

This call for linguistic precision does not mean that children must be taught formal grammar and rhetoric, but a detailed classification does imply that children can learn to respond to the signaling systems of language without having conscious knowledge of the existence of formal grammar. It does mean that developers of skills (including teachers) need to be aware of language units.

The next list, collected from at least fifty sources, represents some prerequisites for proficiency in the complex skills of listening. This compendium represents items that should be in both the listener's and the instructor's personal glossary. The list implies vocabulary background, a relevant skill in itself. Some of these ideas, cued by phrases, are common in the literature; others are less so.

A. Skills of attending and tuning out distraction
B. Memory span
    1. Auditory memory span for meaningful sound sequences and syllables
    2. Auditory memory span for nonsense syllables
    3. Auditory memory span for words, sentences, paragraphs, and other linguistic features in organized and unorganized discourse (see section on discriminations)
C. Further elements of a working vocabulary for listening
    1. Hearing and listening (understanding the difference between these terms)
    2. Auding (including levels of listening, showing increase in consciousness and complexity of comprehension and processing skill)
    3. Two-way responsibility for communication
    4. Having a flexible purpose for listening
    5. Optimal use of leftover thinking space (or thinking time) while listening
    6. Similarities and differences between listening and reading (e.g., contexts: person context, time pressure, material or hardware medium)
    7. Empathetic listening
    8. Report versus emotive spoken discourse
    9. Interrelation of other language skills with listening skill
    10. Nonfacilitating barriers or "bad" habits in listening
        a) Labeling the subject as dull (negative attitude)
        b) Overreacting—failure to recognize the nonrational, the subliminal device, letting emotion-laden words get in the way of the message, excessive self-assertion of emotional aspects of the communication atmosphere, personal antagonism
        c) Inflexible purpose, e.g., listening only for details, detailed outlining of all input
        d) Faking attention instead of directing and maintaining it ("tuning out")
        e) Ease of distraction

f) Missing large blocks of the message
g) Listening only to easy material (avoiding challenging listening)
h) Wasting the difference between speech and thought speed
i) Daydreaming
j) Private planning, private parallel argument
k) Creating distractions
l) Inability to anticipate next point (inability to plan for and anticipate the message)
m) Inability to identify supporting material
n) Inability to summarize in own words
o) Inability to relate thinking to main theme of spoken material

11. Using the difference between speech and thought speed (tuning in, turning on)
a) Using related mental imagery, applying criteria, relating past personal experience to the message, entertaining many alternatives, adjusting to differing situations and individuals
b) Identifying focus words or organizational clues or signals, e.g., time signals, tenses, articles
c) Having a question set, i.e., gentle, exploratory probing

12. Discrimination
a) Sound—stress, juncture (pause), pitch (suprasegmental contrasts), cadence, rhythm, emphasis, phrasing, rate, volume
b) Sequence
c) Sound contrasts, e.g., vowel, consonant
d) Grammatical contrasts, e.g., The business fails. The businesses fail.
e) Reduced forms, e.g., You can't jog. You can jog.

13. Using context
a) Short message—without memory (mnemonic) devices
b) Component focus
c) Contextual focus
d) Long message—with mnemonic devices
e) Preparation for listening
(1) Prior discussion of context and/or vocabulary
(2) Giving the number of major points to come

        (3) Giving a partial outline
        (4) Question outline
    f) Selective listening
        (1) Note taking
        (2) Listening for time signals, tenses, articles
        (3) Unguided reconstruction—summary

14. Finding the organizational skeleton in the spoken discourse
15. Avoiding the illusion that expression is communication
16. Knowing group discussion rules, strategies, and courtesies
17. Demanding meaning (conscious effort to increase vocabulary)
18. Encouraging upward communication (for a person in authority)
19. Using redundancy to reduce line loss
20. Avoiding overset for redundancy (Teacher always repeats directions many times, so why bother to listen the first time?)
21. Improving the climate for communication
22. Making a listening inventory
23. Keeping a listening log
24. Constructing standards for effective listening
25. Appreciating unexpressed meanings (rarely do we say exactly what we mean or mean exactly what we say)
26. Understanding the concept of noise pollution
27. Listening appreciatively: sensing emotions, moods, manner of delivery
28. Listening with patience
29. Listening with diversity of response
30. Listening with flexibility in using concrete and abstract thinking
31. Listening nonegocentrically
32. Listenability (related to readability; see Glasser, 1975)
33. Getting horizontal transfer from listening skills to reading and the reverse
34. Listening critically
    a) Evaluating hearsay evidence
    b) Evaluating hidden assumptions in oral speech
    c) Evaluating point of view
    d) Spotting and evaluating speaker's purpose, intent

The next step after formulating some dimensions for a taxonomy of skills might be to choose for instructional emphasis those of cultural importance and of particular relevance to the target group's age level, attention span, and diagnosed weaknesses. Although cross-sectional and longitudinal studies indicate step-wise growth, they tell little else about selection and placement of skills other than what common sense and a knowledge of child development already indicate. Perhaps the worst error has been to underestimate the vocabulary, grasp of language, and complexity of the thinking process that even the youngest child in school has.

The following material is an example of skills or objectives selected for a fifth-grade population in a number of Southern California counties (Lundsteen, 1969). Block diagrams and a description of a tentative hierarchy of some general listening skills and some critical listening skills are included. Chapter four touches on the measurement that was used to assess these skills.

Tentative Hierarchy of Some General and Critical Listening Skills

A designer of an instructional hierarchy[10] usually determines the final tasks for the child and then asks the question: "What does the child need to be able to do to perform this task successfully?" Then an objective is added. This procedure is continued with each subordinate objective eventually defining a hierarchy of objectives extending to the entering or prerequisite skills for the child in this program. Accompanying the block diagrams are lists of objectives for pupil behavior in a more complete statement, the numbers corresponding to the diagram. This material gives the teacher a quick overview of the behaviors to be exhibited and evaluated. The two hierarchies presented in this chapter are a supporting one for general listening (Figure 10) and one for critical listening (Figure 11). (Also see Weaver and Rutherford, 1974, for an extensive hierarchical listing of listening skills from the prenatal stage to grades four through six.)

Verbs are important components in stating objectives. Some of the major verbs in these objectives are adapted from the work at the Southwest Regional Laboratory in Inglewood, California, as found in a paper by Baker and others (1968): (1) identifying, (2) naming, (3) ordering, (4) describing, and (5) constructing. The verb *construct* as used here reflects a verbal product produced autonomously by the child but guided by criteria rather than by a concrete object designed and assembled. *Identify* is nonverbal in response while *name* is verbal; *describe* includes recall or identification of characteristics.

An objective in the hierarchies may include several of the verbs, especially if the verb applies to the last and perhaps most complex behavior, *constructing*. During a lesson the same objective may call for all five action levels—calling for a response in which child

behavior varies from pointing to a word on the board to constructing on his or her own revised criteria for evaluating hypotheses.

The prerequisites may be initially possessed by the child at a
relatively low level because these prerequisites continue to operate
and to be reinforced, interrelated, and practiced as the hierarchies
progress.

Subskill: General Listening Objectives (Fig. 10)

1. Distinguishing Hearing from Listening (prerequisite). For
   example, the child identifies, names, describes, discriminates nonverbal and incomprehensible sounds in contrast
   to verbal messages that he or she comprehends.

2. Demonstrating Two-way, Listener-Speaker Responsibility
   (prerequisite). The child names, describes, distinguishes
   (true-false questions), demonstrates (e.g., during "bring-
   and-brag" time), constructs, applies, and states principle of
   responsibility for two-way communication.

3. Selecting Facts and Details. Given four possible choices
   after listening to a selection, the child recalls and identifies
   facts and details within the selection.

4. Sequential Ordering. The child recalls and identifies sequential order; responds to such questions as, "Which
   came first in the story?" The idea is to know what you are
   doing, where you are going, and why.

5. Selecting Main Idea. The child recalls verbal information
   and orders, distinguishes, constructs, and identifies the
   main idea from among the four choices given.

6. Summarizing. Covertly, the child recalls, describes, details,
   distinguishes, orders many main ideas, and overtly identifies a summary statement from among four choices given;
   responds to questions such as, "Which title best covers all
   of the ideas in the story?" or "Give one sentence telling
   what the story is about."

7. Relating One Idea to Another. The child recalls, describes
   details, distinguishes, summarizes (all covertly), and overtly identifies a valid relationship from among four choices;
   responds to questions such as, "Finding a cobra was related to which of these ideas?"

8. Inference Making. Covertly, the pupil recalls, describes
   details, distinguishes, orders, summarizes, identifies relationships, and overtly identifies a correct inference from
   among four choices; responds, for example, to "The story
   leads us to believe that . . ."

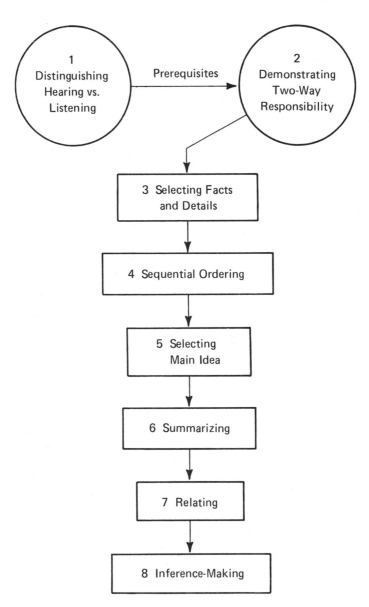

Fig. 10. A tentative learning hierarchy of general listening objectives.

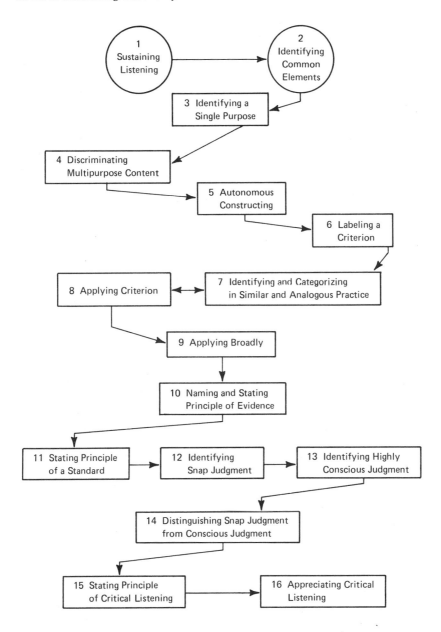

Fig. 11. A tentative learning hierarchy for critical listening.

Subskill: Critical Listening Objectives (Fig. 11)

1. Sustaining Listening (prerequisite). The child listens all the way to the end of the message; for example, she or he identifies and discriminates meanings in periodic sentences and surprising last words which are embedded in lessons for prerequisite testing purposes.

2. Identifying Common Elements (prerequisite). The child identifies a component within an example in which a speaker gives experimental fact, historical fact, or observational fact; plays on words, uses exaggeration or surprise; or "paints" a funny word picture.

3. Identifying a Single Purpose. The child listens critically (applies criterion or judges in light of criteria) to a message with supposedly one purpose.

4. Listening Critically to Multipurpose Content. The child listens critically (applies standard or criterion) to a longer message with several purposes, e.g., to give facts, to persuade, and to be humorous.

5. Autonomous Constructing. The child constructs examples of his or her own.

6. Labeling Criteria. The child names and stores the preceding common elements found in the formulating of facts or of humorous discourse as a set of classes and as criteria for later use in judgment.

7. Identifying and categorizing Fact and Discourse, Opinion or Humor in Similar and in Analogous Practice. Given an example, the child names "giving facts" or "being funny" as a speaker's purpose and can tell criteria used and the details that fit criteria.

8. Applying Criteria. The child applies criteria when listening to mixed examples in order to match the message with a main purpose—to be factual, funny, or to give opinion (in a recognition situation).

9. Applying Broadly. The child applies criteria to reported "on-your-own" experiences outside of the class lesson time.

10. Naming and Stating Principle of Evidence. The child names and states the principle of noticing evidence in order to apply criteria. (There must be evidence or reasons to back up judgments, e.g., elements of facts or of humor.)

11. Stating Principle of a Standard. The child states the principle of using or creating a standard by which to judge. (There must be a standard used consciously when judging, e.g., related to discrimination of humor.)

12. Identifying and Naming Snap Judgment. Given examples, the child names elements of behavior indicating snap judgment (e.g., did not listen all the way to the end, did not notice evidence, did not use or cannot name and apply a standard).

13. Identifying and Naming Highly Conscious Judgment. Given examples, the child names elements of behavior demonstrating highly conscious judgment (e.g., listening all the way to the end of the message, noticing evidence or details of humor, naming and applying a standard).

14. Distinguishing Snap Judgment from Highly Conscious Judgment. The child identifies, names, describes, and distinguishes between snap judgment or opinion and highly conscious or reflective judgment when presented oral, train-of-thought examples of each.

15. Stating Principle of Critical Listening. The child describes the principle of or defines critical listening in his or her own words, including *evidence, standard,* and *highly conscious judgment,* or words similar in meaning, and tells the function of each.

16. Appreciating Critical Listening to Speaker's Purpose. Given illustrative examples, the child expresses or states the "principle" to the effect that "If you don't listen critically, you may be fooled or miss a lot of fun." Observation of behavior in class and lessons, including discussion, demonstrates acceptance and even preference for critical listening (but in a way that does not antagonize and block further communication).

It may seem from the foregoing analyses and lists that stress is laid solely on the solitary listener and the cognitive domain. However, the interactive and the affective domains—the next topic—have not been forgotten.

What Are Some Skills of Empathy and Role-Taking?

Another dimension of listening skills should be examined: the development of role-taking and empathy in children—the social-interpersonal skills used in listening. This set of skills has two parts: (1) The ability to "take the role" of other persons, or intended listeners by assessing their capacities, i.e., their needs, intentions, opinions, strengths, and limitations—emotional, perceptual, or intellectual; and (2) the ability to use this grasp of the attributes of others as a tool in communicating effectively with them.[11]

Listening is like a two-sided mirror, one side reflecting the expresser, the other side the receiver. Children progress toward this understanding as their listening becomes less self-centered. The young child is at first egocentric, the prisoner of his or her own individual perspective, largely ignorant of and unconcerned with the perspectives of others.[12]

There are descriptive features of role-taking that take it beyond the listening skills mentioned earlier. Role-takers may base their estimate of listener attributes and capabilities on: (1) past general knowledge and expectations of people and their behavior; and (2) present perception according to the listener's apparent behavior.[13] For example, how did the audience respond? Were they blindfolded? From what position, physically, are they seeing a person or object? This socialized, other-person-oriented communication has been variously called *role-taking, role perception, role-playing* (or *enactment*), silently *putting yourself in someone else's shoes,* and *empathy. Empathy,* preferable to *role-taking,* implies more of a feeling tone (although not quite so much as *sympathy*); that is, one's own identity and objectivity are maintained. Moreover, the information is definitely not gathered to provide a tool for a manipulative, persuasive purpose in the sense of taking unfair advantage of the listener.

There are other aspects of role-taking. The exercise of this set of skills may occur briefly or continue over a long period of time. This discrimination is important in helping the communicator to make an appropriate response—a simplified definition of "a person who listens well." This set of interactive skills takes the communicator beyond the A, B, C's of passive listening (*A*cuity, *B*asic discrimination, and *C*omprehension) to a way of doing something about messages in the most socially appropriate way.

Egocentric and Nonegocentric Communication

To clarify the concept of role-taking still further, we need to briefly explore the distinction between egocentric and nonegocentric communication.[14] Egocentric communication, in its simplest form, consists of only two steps:

1. The *speaker* apprehends events and codes them internally so that they are meaningful to him or her.

2. The *speaker* sends the *listener* a message about the events. The message has not been changed to suit the attributes of the *listener,* but is essentially the same message the *speaker* coded for himself or herself. Thus, it is an egocentric communication.

Nonegocentric communication has an extra step and the continuing dimension of holding in mind the relevant attributes of the listener. The first step is the same for both egocentric and non-egocentric communication. Accordingly, notice the different second step.

1. The *speaker* apprehends events and codes them for himself or herself.

2. Before and during the *speaker's* communication to the *listener,* the *speaker* attempts to discriminate those attributes of his or her *listener* that appear to be pertinent to the *listener's* ability to decode the *speaker's* message about the events.

3. With this information in mind, the *speaker* recodes the events as a message he or she thinks is appropriate for the *listener's* needs. The *speaker* may have to actively suppress the tendency to allow his or her message to drift or regress to the egocentric error of coding just for himself or herself.

The following are a few thoughts on the applicability of these models to other language arts and to the various aims of discourse. Research in this area has been focused on oral communication. But the roles discussed above could be related to written and to gesture messages (kinesics) as well. Of course, should the listener attributes which are relevant to the events for the message be the same for both speaker and listener, the recoding step would, ideally, not be needed. However, this coinciding of attributes and aims (e.g., the same vocabulary meanings, the same perspective) appears relatively late. The *aim* (or use) of the communication involved might be partially self-expressive, informative, literary, or persuasive. Studies have dealt mainly with informative aims (such as instructing a blindfolded person on how to play a game).

A few tasks, however, were definitely persuasive, such as the one in which the child was instructed to try to sell her or his listener a tie or a TV set.[15]

One of Flavel's tasks was #ID, where a child sees, and tells a story about, a series of seven pictures involving a boy, an apparently fierce dog, and an apple tree. Then three pictures are removed from the series. Next, the child's second examiner enters the room, and the child is requested to predict the story that the new examiner would probably tell from the remaining four pictures, assuming that she or he has never seen the whole series. The pictures are so-constructed that the complete series suggests a story quite different from the one depicted by the four remaining pictures, because in the remaining pictures there is no direct hint of the fierce dog. The goal is to see if the child can suppress her or his own perspective in favor of predicting that of her or his prospective partner in communication and to see if the child can tell the story accurately from the other point of view. Child responses were placed in one of four categories, according to sensitivity to the role-taking aspects of the task.

Who, Then, Is the Most Skilled Listener?

Considering all the dimensions to the skill of listening, it is clear that the skill involves much more than mere auditory discrimination. Beyond acuity of hearing, listening comprehension involves such matters as attention span, memory storage including retention of mental images or pictures, vocabulary, the organization and retrieval of facts, and the understanding of the speaker's purpose. Moreover, there are the additional mental activities of searching and testing background knowledge, of recognizing linguistic features, and of developing sets of empathy or role-taking. Again, the "best" listener in any group (with respect to skills in general and to literal comprehension) *is the person who most consistently, in the least time and in the greatest variety of circumstances, most closely comprehends the speaker's meaning in the widest variety of spoken material.*[16] From this writer's point of view, the "best listener" is also capable of using his or her listening skill with the *widest range of thinking processes.* This range progresses from simple association to highly complex conscious, creative, critical, and problem-oriented processes. The range goes from one-way intake to complex feedback systems for the interpersonal meeting of minds. In brief, the most skilled listener makes the best sense out of sound and uses the product appropriately. Finally, superior performance in listening skill probably not only requires possession of a wide range of basic competencies, but also the ability to *mobilize* them for a particular communicative situation and then to apply them beyond the listening moment.

This chapter has presented some past and current ideas concerning a taxonomy of listening skills, the dimensions of these skills, their prerequisites, ways of classifying them, a "brainstorming" of considerations, and a suggested method for formulating skills into learner objectives and arranging them in tentative hierarchies. Examples designed to encourage further thought about and generation of objectives appropriate to a target population of learners were given. Still one of the most complete sources for a compendium of listening skills is the book by Russell and Russell (1959), *Listening Aids through the Grades.* This manual arranges 190 activities into 3 levels, kindergarten, primary, and intermediate, and goes from general to simple and specific to more complex.

Additional Activities to Promote Listening Comprehension

The teacher can use this series of listening comprehension tasks for problem solving at least as early as kindergarten (in many cases earlier) or can adapt them for higher grade levels. A "Listening-to-Solve Kit" should be compiled for a learning center and contain audio tapes, pictures, and pupil-response materials.

In general, help children to welcome problems to solve because they become lessons that make us better people. "Better people" means more grown up, smarter or less ignorant, better to be with, and more in control of self and one's environment. Guide the children to see that listening well helps them to comprehend each of the following tasks in the problem-solving process.[17]

Listening to be aware that a problem exists. Tell the children a story in which a problem is implicit and see if they can sense it. Example: "One day a little girl found a kitten. She'd always wanted one. Taking it home, she started in the door with it. Her mother, standing in the doorway, pointed back outside. Does the girl have a problem? What is it? What questions would you need to ask?"

Listening for implications and consequences in a problem. After describing a situation to the children, the teacher asks what might happen. The comprehension task is to predict multiple consequences. Situations might be: "Your mother and your teacher meet on the street. They start to talk about you. What are some things they might say?" Or, "Two children are arguing over something (e.g., whose turn it is at the painting easel or what TV program to watch). What might they say?" Or the teacher might say, "Suppose there are three little shelves on which to put all of the paints, pans for mixing them, water jars, and brushes. And suppose the person you are teaching to clean up piled them all on one shelf. What might happen: (1) the cabinet might fall over, (2) the shelf might break under the load, (3) the boxes might not fit, (4) some other possibility?"

Listening to get the facts before solving a problem. Deliberately give the children unclear directions to see if they listen and ask for clearer ones. For example: Place a piece of paper, a piece of chalk, and a crayon in front of a child. Then say: "Pick *it* up, please."

Listening to state the problem and to suggest creative hypotheses. There will be plenty of opportunities in any classroom for asking children what the problem is and what they think they might do to solve it. It is crucial that the problem be important, interesting, and relevant to the child's experience. For example: "Suppose a child in our class was visiting another class member on Saturday, and they decided that it would be fun to bake some cookies that they could bring to our class for morning snack the next Monday. What problem(s) will they have and what should they do? What else? Are there other smaller problems? Have you thought of as many parts as you can and of the ideas they give you for solving? What might be the most unusual thing they could do? Can you think of a way(s) to solve it that most children would not think of? Just suppose your unusual idea were possible. How could it be?" (To get "unstuck" during solving when you run out of ideas, look at the problem in a new and different way.)

Listening to determine if data are missing. After giving children a problem to solve, ask them what else they need to know before they can solve it. For example, in the earlier problem about the cookies for the class snack, they might need: (1) money, (2) the teacher's permission, and (3) to be sure no one else gets the same idea, or there would be too much to eat before lunch. Suppose the children get the teacher's permission, but no one else has offered any facts. Do the children have all the facts they need to solve the problem? (No; what about the money?) "What other important parts could there be? Have you missed any other important parts of this problem?" How would the children go about finding out what they need to know? What part should they work on first? Or, another example: "Suppose some of your friends tell you that they have found a purse and want you to help them decide what to do with it. Before you could help them decide, what would you need to know?"

Listening to plan procedures creatively. Give the children a problem and ask them to develop a plan for solving it. Example: "Suppose you wanted to teach a friend, who was absent when we learned to do it, how we clean up the paint corner. What would be a good teaching plan? What would you tell or have him or her do first? What next? What would be the most unusual way(s) to teach him or her, a way that most children would not think of? How could this way be used?" Lead the children to think whether their plans will result in action that achieves the goal.

Listening to set a standard for evaluating solutions. After giving the children a description of a child solving a problem or carrying out a task, ask at what point the child can tell that she or he has been successful. Example: "This small boy is learning to get his clothes on in the morning all by himself. How will he know if he has dressed himself right?" Or, "This girl is learning to set the dining room table. How will she know she has done it the right way, all by herself?" (Encourage the child to plan evaluatively rather than simply asking an adult authority, such as the mother.) "Suppose she wants to know without having to ask her mother?" (Check ideas with the facts.) "What could she look at or observe?"

Listening to determine if the solution is what the solver intended. Example: "A boy's goal is to have his father bring him a dog he saw on a visit to the dog pound. He wants this dog for a pet, but he can't go get it himself. The dog he wants has long, dark ears, short legs, a short tail, and two spots on its side." Then draw or show the children a picture of the dog the father brought home. "Did the boy get the dog he wanted?" See if the children can notice that only one specification was met and that there is a discrepancy.

After you have collected the children's responses to these tasks that involve "Listen-Comprehend-Solve," you can share them, perhaps scale them, and let the children compare them to the responses made by other children their own age. The children can see alternatives they did not think of and will probably reach farther the next time as a result of studying these models. Encourage children to produce their own "solving-provoking" examples and stories.[18]

The road to good listening. This is a suggested on-going activity that motivates listening improvement and helps children to keep a record of attained concepts and successes. Introduced some time after the first lessons in a unit, the "road" activity may be highly individualized but with some general suggestions. Or the "road" may be a large class or group project. General suggestions for pupils:

> You are about to begin an exciting trip on the road to good listening. Watch out!
>
> 1. On your road draw in "roadblocks" to listening.[19]
>
> 2. Extend your drawing of the winding road. Mark it off in sections.
>
> 3. Think back to your last listening activity. Mark through a section in your road for each success and label them. For example, did you contribute anything to the last class discussion? If so, mark through the next section in the road and give it a label. Use this road to keep a record of your listening successes and to list in words and pictures the ideas about listening that you want to remember. Have fun and good traveling.

4 Are There Methods for Evaluating Listening?

This chapter examines criticisms and rationales applicable to listening tests, including standardized tests, unpublished tests, publishers' informal assessments that accompany their instructional materials, and other informal devices, such as coding sheets, standards, and checklists. Information in this chapter is intended to increase the reader's sensitivity to the quality and variety of available techniques.

Testing: Who Needs It?

Tests help teachers discover and nurture talent; tests also help teachers to select appropriate instructional strategies to use with those children most in need of help. If educational testing were abandoned, excellence in programs would become less tangible, and decisions on important issues of curriculum and method would be made less on the basis of evidence and more on the basis of prejudice and caprice. Testing can erase doubts, justify pride in hard-earned accomplishment, indicate need for advancement, and keep instructional programs up to date and efficient.

Those educators whose values and understandings cause them to advocate listening instruction want methods of determining which skills children possess, which ones they still need to master, and what they are learning, if anything, as a result of new materials, activities, and teaching strategies. Even before clear theoretical and statistical evidence showed that there are separate listening abilities, some researchers had attempted to measure them. The lack of an integrated, conceptual framework for listening meant that these tests lacked agreement in what they measured. Some researchers (who are not noted for reticence in criticism) have sharply condemned all of the measurement attempts, though none of them seriously wants to stop the effort. Measuring hidden behavior by making inferences from responses is a rather frustrating challenge, but it is such an interesting goal that some are still willing to risk failure and ridicule to carry on the attempt.

Some Criticisms

Probably all empirical research on the growth and attainment of listening skills has rested upon observation or upon tests of performance—a special variety of observation. In constructing listening tests, it is difficult to avoid extraneous cues that help individuals to respond in desired ways, or that hinder them or introduce artificiality (see Carroll, 1968). For example, it is likely that in testing situations some of the "best" listeners may have high mental ability but are normally inattentive under nontest circumstances. Others simply do poorly in a test environment. (See Kelly, 1967.) Another and deplorable extraneous factor in tests of mental ability is cultural bias. Studies as early as Smith's (1956) found cultural bias to be as great a negative factor in listening tests as in reading tests.

Listening tests may be fragile. They need to be at the precise and optimal level of difficulty for the individuals taking them. For a larger picture we need "live" listening situations in which a child may be examined during a wide range of activities—from boredom to panic. A complete profile may call for highly specific, imaginative—even devious—ways of studying and evaluating listening behavior. Listening tests should also progress toward a finer linguistic analysis of listening competence, but most of them are based on an inadequate rationale of general language skills.

Without testing, however, the teacher does not know if the child is listening productively or unproductively. Equally important, children cannot guide their own learning without some sort of feedback. In relative isolation, repeated exposure to material may give little sense of direction. Children need the opportunity to make responses that show they have listened. Well-designed test questions, tasks, and situations help.

Children also need to be taught the skills of question answering. Bormuth (1969) suggests a unit of instruction composed of (1) the language message, (2) the question, and (3) the response. The point is that both the test questions and the language features are independently difficult. Test design needs to take into account the relative difficulty of various types of linguistic features and also the relative difficulty inherent in various kinds of questions. Test taking has rarely accounted for or given a breakdown of these features. This lack makes interpretation of past test results questionable (see Ebel, 1976).

A Rationale for Testing

Ability in listening comprehension refers to generalized knowledge-acquisition skills exhibited as a consequence of hearing spoken material (this statement is adapted from Bormuth's [1969] general definition of comprehension). Moreover, testing listening comprehension includes not only the processes necessary to obtain information from spoken language, but also the additional skills needed to exhibit that information. An example, as Bormuth suggested, is to answer questions or respond to tasks in a manner that shows what the listening produced for the individual. Listening comprehension refers not only to mere storage and retrieval of language information, but also to transformation and thinking beyond the material (extrapolation) (Marks and Noll, 1967).

Again, the best listener (with respect to general, literal comprehension) in any group is the one who most consistently, in the least time and in the greatest variety of circumstances, most closely approximates the speaker's meaning in the widest variety of spoken material (adapted from Brown, 1954; Carroll, 1968). From this writer's point of view, the best listener is also capable of using his or her listening skills in the widest range of thinking. This range proceeds from simple to highly complex associations. The best listener is, therefore, the one who best makes sense out of sound. Superior performance in listening skill probably not only requires possession of a wide range of basic competencies, but the ability to *mobilize* them for a particular communicative situation as well.

The thesis of this book is that testing should go past literal comprehension to permit evaluation of listener ability to apprehend aesthetically, empathetically, and judiciously. But, admittedly, it is highly questionable that listeners can do so if they cannot comprehend literally.

Achievement tests are different from comprehension tests. Achievement tests for listening indicate how much of the knowledge in a particular spoken selection from a particular subject matter the child can acquire and exhibit. Comprehension tests indicate how well the child can absorb knowledge generally and from what general type of material. This function is not operating in achievement tests, in which subtests are simply grouped by subject. (These ideas are also adapted from material by Bormuth, 1969.)

The primary assumption is that listening ability is a variable, differing according to maturity, intelligence, hearing, interest, subject matter, and command of language, that is, it is learned behavior. A further assumption is that listening ability is measurable; it can be reliably measured by logically valid tests that sample skills in recall and comprehension of the meaning of spoken language, even, according to a classic study by Caffrey (1953), when tests are given by different examiners.

Investigation of some of these assumptions about separate skills or abilities can be done statistically, one technique being factor analysis. While attempting to investigate the domain of listening, Spearritt (1962) was the first to isolate a listening comprehension factor as distinct from the verbal knowledge factor found in written tests (probably skills in reading). That listening comprehension and verbal knowledge factors were correlated to some extent probably reflects common dependence on background knowledge of vocabulary and language structure. The listening comprehension factor was relatively independent of auditory resistance and memory span. Some of the findings of this study at the grade six level have also been supported at the high school level (Caffrey, 1953) and at the adult level (Taylor and others, 1958). Such testing and study at earlier ages and the longitudinal studies needed to establish individual growth curves in these separate factors have not yet been made.

Are There Standardized Tests That Reliably Measure a Child's Listening Progress from Year to Year?

A standardized test is one which has been administered to a pupil sample that represents the market population, and information obtained from the scores is presented to show the range of performances expected from this particular population of users.

A standardized listening test can be used to: (1) assess the range and distribution of listening ability in a particular group so that the degree of difficulty of oral material can be adjusted; (2) determine if the group has learned what is being taught; (3) measure group improvement in listening skill over a specific period; (4) estimate group reading potential; (5) compare reading and listening skills to make the most of the best mode of reception; and (6) test assumptions about, proposals for, and models of listening.

The following are two useful tests for assessing basic listening abilities: the *Illinois Test of Psycholinguistic Abilities* (ITPA) and the *Wepman Auditory Discrimination Test.* ITPA is published by the Institute for Research on Exceptional Children at the University of Illinois. It is used with children between the ages of two-and-one-half and nine. It has subtests relevant to listening: at the representational level, *Auditory Decoding* and *Auditory-Vocal Association;* and at the automatic-sequential level, an "automatic" test, *Auditory-Vocal Automatic Ability,* and a test of "sequencing," *Auditory-Vocal Sequencing.* Carroll (1968) describes this battery and critiques it. The *Wepman Auditory Discrimination Test* (ages five to nine) assesses ability to discriminate changes in frequency, intensity, or pattern of auditory stimuli (see Stern, 1969, for a critique). A child is presented key words in pairs and is asked to say whether the words sound the same or different. (Chapter five of this book mentions other basic ability tests.)

The *Brown-Carlsen Listening Comprehension Test* is the standardized, pioneer effort in the comprehension field. Although initially designed to be used in grades nine to thirteen, it can also be used at college and post-college levels. The seventy-eight items are grouped in five parts: (1) Immediate Recall, (2) Following Directions, (3) Recognizing Transitions (i.e., Is a sentence in a speech introductory, transitional, concluding, or none of these?), (4) Recognizing Word Meanings (ten items), and (5) Lecture Comprehension (twelve minutes of continuous discourse). For the lecture comprehension section one factor analysis reported by Bateman and others revealed two other factors: (1) listening for details and (2) drawing inferences (in Duker, 1968). Brown (1949) suggested that ability to follow context clues appeared to be the single best test for separating "good" listeners from "poor" ones. The caution and criticism mentioned at the beginning of this chapter also apply to this test.

The *STEP Listening Test* is an attempt by the Educational Testing Service to measure listening comprehension by using the series called the Sequential Tests of Educational Progress. The test appears to be built on the definition "Listening is what happens when people are spoken to" (Kelly, 1967, rebuts this definition). There are two alternate forms for each of four levels: Level 1 (college), Level 2 (grades ten, eleven, twelve), Level 3 (grades seven, eight, nine), and Level 4 (grades four, five, six).

The ninety items suitable for the elementary grades are reported to measure: (1) Plain-sense Comprehension (identifying main ideas, remembering details and simple sequences of ideas, understanding word meanings); (2) Interpretation (understanding implications of main ideas and significant details, interrelationships among ideas, and connotative meanings of words); (3) Evaluation and Application (judging validity of ideas, distinguishing fact from fancy, noting contradictions, e.g., "judging whether the speaker has created the intended mood or effect"). The test items require not only understanding of the spoken discourse but also a wide range of prior knowledge and reasoning abilities.

Criticisms of this test refer to its mix of reading and listening. Also, many of the printed items on the test can be answered by pupils who have not heard the oral material.

There are three possible results from using a comprehension test: (1) the child knows the answer whether or not she or he is exposed to the material; (2) the child can select the correct alternative as a result of having been exposed to the material; (3) the child neither already knows the correct alternative nor learns it from exposure (Marks and Noll, 1967). Only knowledge obtained as a consequence of listening to the oral test passage actually represents listening comprehension. It is difficult to find a passage containing information about which a child knows absolutely nothing. But the *STEP* test appears to contain many questions that a child can answer without listening to the test passage. Spearritt (1962) deleted many of these items after pre-testing the questions on a pilot sample without the stimulus passages when he used the test in his study. (Further information and critique is given by Carroll, 1968.)

The Educational Testing Service added listening tests to the *Cooperative Primary Tests* (1967). There are two forms for grades one and two and for grades two and three for unspeeded assessment. The teacher reads words, sentences, stories, expositions, and poems. The child demonstrates his or her comprehension by marking appropriate pictures. In this test, listening includes more than receiving the spoken word; it includes identifying illustrative or associated instances, recalling elements, interpreting the ideas presented, and drawing inferences. The time required is about thirty-five minutes. A typical item is "I went for a ride," with picture options of a child swimming, a child walking, and a car. The handbook encourages instructional-diagnostic use of local-item analysis data for groups of children.

The *Durrell Listening-Reading Series* (group test) is designed to provide a comparison of children's reading and listening abilities. Revised in 1969, this Harcourt Brace Jovanovich publication seeks to assess both vocabulary and sentence comprehension at three levels, roughly grades 1-3.5, 3.5-6, and 7-9. The optional responses are also administered orally so that the child does no reading that would confound the performance. The series is reported to measure the degree of retardation in reading as compared to listening.

In 1973 Harcourt released the *Durrell-Sullivan Reading Capacity Test,* which Durrell envisioned as a listening test for preschool and primary students and as an instrument for estimating a child's potential capacity for learning to read. The *Murphy-Durrell Reading Readiness Analysis* for beginning first grade (also published by Harcourt) includes subtests on auditory discrimination (phonemes in initial and final positions).

What Cautions Must Be Observed?

Test validity depends on an appropriate match between the sample of tested content or skills and the objectives of the instructional program. If the test does not measure the listening skills introduced in the program but measures skills developed later, the scores will fail to show the effects of teaching. This lack of a match has occurred in many experiments that were designed to teach listening but did not produce positive results. But, just as unfortunately, if the teaching is merely to provide competence for the test, the test results will be biased. When teachers are under pressure to show high achievement scores for their classes, standardized tests may be invalidly used.

The test score of a single child reflects a sizable error of measurement. At the high and low ends of the distribution of scores, one or two wrong (or right) guesses greatly change the grade-level equivalent score. Group tests measure achievement of groups, not individuals—particularly over a year or less. School people misuse group-achievement test scores when they use them to determine the placement of individual children. Another caution: avoid comparing groups that were not represented in the population from which the test norms were developed.

The teacher's question at the beginning of this section was "Is there any standard that a teacher can refer to that will enable him or her to determine a child's progress in listening from year to year?" In light of the preceding discussion, we can say that standardized, norm-referenced tests are not the answer. Tests especially designed for administration to individuals give a more accurate assessment. However, an inordinate amount of testing—often required by individual measurement—with the tensions that usually accompany it, may rob the child of instructional time and create an unhappy classroom atmosphere.

What Are Criterion-Referenced Tests?

Criterion-referenced tests appear to have entered the classroom more recently than standardized, norm-referenced tests. A criterion-referenced test is designed to determine whether or not a pupil can perform a defined task. For example, when a child listens to material of a certain length and complexity, is she or he able to identify the main idea in nine out of ten items? Criterion-referenced tests are used to make short-range instructional decisions and to see how well the teacher's own instructional objectives are being achieved by the students. Instead of a score based on the number of questions answered correctly, a criterion-referenced test yields a listing of objectives attained (Ebel, 1976).

Actually, a further description of criterion-referenced tests reveals that they are nothing new. Examples are such work-sample tests as typing, where the score is determined in terms of words typed per minute. But if those typing scores are compared to those made by other people, the test is norm-referenced.

Criterion-referenced test givers make inferences about the on-the-job behavior of those taking their tests. They hope that every person answers or performs correctly on all test items (or answers a certain set percentage correctly). Thus they hope that every person will receive the same score on the criterion-behavior (e.g., one hundred on the spelling test before trying to learn any more new words). This lack of variability is not the aim of norm-referenced tests, which are designed to discriminate among those who know and those who do not.

Criterion-referenced tests are most useful in producing inferences when the behavior sought is obvious and simple. This kind of observation has been with us for a long time. Criterion-referenced tests focus on much more complete attainment of a much smaller number of objectives. This focus may be advantageous when the tester is dealing with the mastery of simple basic skills. Whether it is equally desirable in other areas of learning (such as complex listening comprehension skills) is open to question (Ebel, 1976).

Unpublished Tests

A worthwhile source of ideas for assessing listening is the unpublished theses and dissertations in which tests have not been carried beyond one or two revisions. (The Brown-Carlsen test was once one of these measures.) Examples are mentioned in reviews by Russell (1964), Duker (1969), and Lundsteen (1969a). The Duker (1968) annotated bibliography shows sixty-five entries on unpublished tests.

One interesting measure is a Spanish Listening Comprehension Test designed to evaluate elementary Spanish television instruction for grades four and six (Anastasiow and Espinosa, 1966). Another source is a large Title III ESEA project in Alameda County, California (Witkin, 1969). Hedrick and Manning developed a measure for the USOE project Programs in Oral Communication, Alameda County, California. (These programs are detailed in chapter five.) During a ten-minute, tape-recorded test, students listen to two speakers giving conflicting instructions simultaneously at different signal/distractions ratios. Students circle or mark with X's certain pictures in their booklets in response to the auditory stimuli.

Another listening test was developed to identify educational potential among disadvantaged junior high school students by using appropriate content. Interviews suggested that this content should include sports, adventure, biographies of heroes, and spy and mystery stories (Orr and Graham, 1968).

Walner (1974) developed a test of listening comprehension for kindergarten and beginning first graders. It contains six graded passages and eighty-four literal and inferential questions. She has dealt with content, criterion-related, and predictive validities and considers the alternate forms and internal reliabilities to be high.

Neville and Pugh (1974) conducted an interesting study that compared children's errors in cloze tests by using a reading modality and a listening modality. Sixty-six children aged nine and ten were tested in two groups with two parallel cloze tests of reading comprehension. The same tests were then given as cloze tests of listening comprehension. Their results were as follows: (1) students did better on the reading cloze test than on the listening cloze test; (2) although certain cloze tests are apparently equivalent measures of reading comprehension, it does not signify that they are necessarily equivalent tests of listening comprehension;

(3) reading modality had an advantage: children were able to adopt a nonsequential approach and use subsequent information to help fill in an earlier blank; if children used the listening modality, they could not do this and were dependent on the preceding information. The blank destroys continuity, organization, intonation (stress, pitch, juncture patterns)—the "melody line" of the speaker's discourse.

An unpublished test of critical listening that matches the skills described in chapter three has been described elsewhere (Lundsteen, 1969 a and b). Subtests are (1) Detecting the Speaker's Purpose (humor, fact, persuasion); (2) Analyzing and Judging Propaganda, and (3) Analyzing and Judging Arguments. This seventy-nine-item test has explicitly stated standards for the child to apply during the judgmental process.

The following is a test example for judging a speaker's purpose. The directions instruct children in using a criterion for judging; for the test situation itself an arbitrary criterion is furnished.

> A boy is reading a want ad aloud to a crowd of friends: "For sale, big friendly dog. Eats anything. Loves children." What was the speaker's purpose?
>
> 1. To be funny
> 2. To give facts
> 3. To persuade
>
> Mark the number corresponding to your answer choice. (Pause 7 seconds.)

In the section of the test dealing with propaganda there are nine analysis items, (e.g. Which propaganda trick was being employed: bad words, glad words, bandwagon, glittering generalities, transfer, testimonial, plain-folks, cardstacking, side tracking? There are nine judgment items that could be categorized as bad, harmless, good. There are nine reason items: "Would you judge the propaganda as you did because . . . ?" followed by three reasons.) Each propaganda item is subjected to the three types of questions. Here is an example of a test item from the propaganda instrument.

> "Drive carefully; the life you save might be your own."
>
> Question 38: What method is the speaker using to persuade you?
>
> 1. Uses big, general, catchy ideas or slogans that appeal.
> 2. Makes you want to do as others do.
> 3. Gets a famous person to give a talk or testimonial in favor of the idea.
> 4. Uses a tempting idea that does not really belong.
>
> Mark it. (7 seconds)

Question 39: How would you judge this propaganda?

1. bad
2. harmless or neutral
3. good

Mark it. (7 seconds)

Question 40: Because:

1. being too slow in driving can cause just as many accidents as not being careful enough.
2. you can try to remind people to be safe drivers, but you never change people very much.
3. every effort needs to be made to reduce death on our streets and highways.

Mark it. (7 seconds)

Scattered, unpublished tests such as these might be brought together to add to a theoretical framework for the testing of listening. (Also see Wilkinson, 1969, for British tests of personal relationship, varying registers of discourse, and prediction in conversation; and Friedman and Johnson, 1968, for an analysis of a variety of tests to determine their possible use as measures of speeded and unspeeded listening.)

Publishers' Tests That Accompany Listening Materials

Ideas for preparing tests to measure listening skills accompany the instructional materials from many publishers. In 1969 Science Research Associates published the *Listening Skills Program,* which consists of a twenty-four-item pretest and post-test. The pretest is actually a motivational device to give pupils a frame of reference; questions are answered yes or no. Items refer to detecting rhyme, comprehension of details, inferences, sequence, main ideas, facts, and purposes; understandings about the listening act; and following directions. The teacher's manual also has an informal self-rating (answered yes or no) of pupil listening habits that may also be used as a pre- and post-test. Pupils next fill out a listening skills record, listing the items missed on the test. The record will show which recording they should listen to for needed practice; after such practice, the pupils check the recording off the list. Pupil-teacher conferences are encouraged. The teacher's guide gives ideas for extended practice. (Test data are not reported.) Instructional material is multilevel and multiskill for grades four, five, and six and supposedly includes instruction on cause and effect and on creative and critical listening with the help of tape, record, or cassette.

An earlier SRA publication is a series of Listening Skill Builders which is part of the *Reading Laboratory Series.* Testing follows each teacher-read lesson, and pupils enter results on progress charts in the pupil books.

Other listening measurement materials are found, for example, in the *Botel Reading Inventory,* where the Word Opposites Test may be given as both a listening test and a reading test. *My Weekly Reader* contains listening comprehension tests for diagnosis and practice. At primary levels pupils mark pictures; at upper-grade levels the pupils write a direct answer usually calling for factual recall. Other programs, some of which contain some means of formal evaluation, are mentioned in the next chapter on materials. (See also the *Kindergarten Auditory Screening Test,* published by Follett. Using a phonograph record, the test measures (1) listening against noise, (2) synthesizing phonemes into words, and (3) determining whether or not paired words are identical.)

Tests that accompany listening materials, unpublished tests, and standardized tests can all serve as models for the teacher's own development of evaluation instruments. With awareness gained from familiarity with these measures, the teacher may gain insight into his or her own listening skills, *especially if the teacher actually takes parts of these tests.* (See chapter five of this book for tests of auditory discrimination that accompany programs.)

How Can the Teacher Use Informal Devices?

Much information about needs and growth can be obtained by both pupil and teacher. One method is to pinpoint significant behavior (seek feedback), select appropriate time samples, tally with a wrist counter or with marks on a piece of tape, and keep records of progress (charting). In addition to the pupil-teacher observations, class logs, diaries, and anecdotal records also furnish survey material on amounts of time spent and provide data for classifying listening purposes and behaviors. Individual and small-group conferences and pupil pairs are useful for making evaluation highly relevant. As the class gradually records desirable listening behaviors, they turn them into class standards, which can be formalized as checklists. A sample checklist, developed in a class where students wished to eliminate certain listening problems, is shown in Figure 12.

Checklist of Listening Roadblocks

Check
here

Hearing

1. I often have trouble hearing what people say. ( )
2. The speaker talked too softly. ( )
3. The speaker talked loudly enough, but not clearly. ( )
4. The room was too noisy:
   The noise came from (a) people around me ( )
                     (b) outside the building ( )
                     (c) the hall ( )
                     (d) other sources ( )
                        (explain)

Listening

1. I didn't pay attention because I wasn't interested. ( )
2. I didn't pay attention because I was thinking
   about what I was going to say. ( )
3. The speaker or sounds began before I got settled. ( )
4. I was thinking about other things (explain). ( )
5. I missed some and could not figure out what was going on. ( )
6. I got wrapped up like a cocoon in my own argument
   and planning. ( )
7. I couldn't understand, so I quit listening. ( )
   a. I couldn't find anything I already knew about to match
   up with what was said. ( )
   b. I couldn't summarize in my own words. ( )
8. It was hard to keep up because I couldn't figure out what
   might come next. ( )
9. I listened like a sponge. I got so concerned with details I
   could not tell the main part from what was just supporting. ( )

Vocabulary

1. These words or sounds were new to me: (1) _____
   (2) _____ (3) _____ (4) _____ (5) _____
2. I thought the word _____ meant _____

Skills or things I think I do well in when I'm listening or am showing
improvement in are:

Fig. 12. A checklist of listening roadblocks can help students identify and
solve listening problems.

Coding Schemes

The teacher can incorporate valuable discussion behaviors into coding devices. They are then mimeographed and given to pupils. This type of material (and the standards) are best built up bit by bit, inductively, with the children, who then genuinely understand the material and feel that it exists partly by their choice. Figure 13 is an example of seven items for general listening; Figure 14 presents a sample lesson plan.

Teachers can also use children's graded texts and published paragraphs for various grade levels to form a diagnostic tool usually called an informal reading inventory. Instead of determining oral *reading* and comprehension level (as indicated by the most difficult selection read successfully by the child), the teacher can read aloud to the child the paragraphs in the inventory. Then by asking questions on the content the teacher can determine the highest level at which the pupil can understand material when it is spoken. Such an informal device is helpful in getting a general idea of the level of listening comprehension of a child who is linguistically different from others in the class.

If the listener's first task is to recreate in his or her mind the "meaning" of the speaker, then a profitable assessment activity is to have the children write their own passages for listening tests. Children can thereby have a hand in designing the questions to be asked about their passages. In this way the child becomes the best authority on what the passage means and can settle conflicts of opinion that might arise.

Questions

Bormuth (1969) elaborated common types of questions that are thought to assess literal comprehension; among them are the "Rote Wh- questions" (who, which, what). He shows that by using nonsense words, this type of question does not test semantic comprehension with any certainty, but it does form a base for questions that do.

For example, given a sentence containing the nonsense words *The piabarn ploshed into the wormstruffle,* even young children can answer "wh- questions" such as "Who ploshed into the wormstruffle?" The answer, *the piabarn,* implies that, in some situations, questions of this type do not necessarily require that the child comprehend word meaning. The structure of the first sentence is something similar to *The girl jumped into the spaghetti,* or, more likely, *the swimming pool.* Bormuth mentions questions

Coding Responses of Listeners

Guide I

1. TW: Two-way responsibility

2. D: Details

3. Se: Sequence

4. M Id: Main Ideas

5. S: Summary

6. R: Relationship

7. T: Transfer

Fig. 13. A sample coding sheet for listening behavior. See Figure 14 for a lesson plan that employs the coding sheet.

Lesson Plan for Coding a Taped Discussion

Challenge to Pupils (Learner Objective)

Identify, name, and describe aspects of listening by coding parts of a taped discussion.

Materials

Guide(s) for each pupil, "Coding Responses of Listeners"; taped segment of class discussion for coding; paper and pencil for pupils

Suggested Steps

1. Distribute coding sheet to pupils.
2. Discuss the coding sheet and check class understanding of the behaviors listed.
3. Play a segment of a tape recording of a class discussion.
4. Use the coding sheet as a guide.
5. Encourage the children to ask questions.
6. Discuss elements of listening behavior inferred from the responses (or lack of response) on the tape.
7. Replay the tape segment to verify the coding and confirm inferences by checking with the listener whose response is being examined.
8. Have pupils tabulate the frequency of occurrence of various items on the coding guide.
9. Pupils can then determine the desirable responses that have low or no occurrence and try to plan for more practice or situations that would elicit responses.
10. Once familiar with the procedure, children can repeat these steps in small groups, which they direct themselves.

Fig. 14. A sample lesson plan for identifying listening behaviors in class discussion.

that encourage the respondent to comprehend the antecedents of later expressed ideas and intersentence relationships, a three-stage procedure of designing. His analysis emphasizes the neglected linguistic features of questions.

Questions used in the Thinking Improvement Project (mentioned earlier) are designed to (1) help the teacher probe during discussion for readiness, (2) induce reinforcement, and (3) provoke elements that promote transfer (Lundsteen, 1968, 1976b). This analysis attempts to emphasize the psychological-instructional features of questions. The sample below shows a suggested hierarchy of questions and the teaching-learning approach that the discussion questions were designed to promote. (See Lundsteen, 1976b, for sample lesson plans using this approach.)

Suggested Question Hierarchy	Teaching-Learning Approach (Matching Concepts)
Readiness or Motivation (Subconcepts)	
What did you notice? What stood out for you?	Openness, verbal fluency, activation (all responses recorded for all to see)
To check up, what does this mean to you now?	Diagnosis of pupil boundaries of concepts
What did you hear? Could you listen to that? Can you tell us what you think?	Subskills
Let's pretend that it's not just us, but anyone in the whole world. What then?	Activation
Who could these listeners be? When? Where? How many places? How? For what reasons? Why?	Facts and conditions
Can more of you recall? What else? Mary? . . . Paul? . . . Sam? . . . Now see if we can take these little ideas and put them into larger groups. Jean? . . . Adam? . . . Mamie? . . .	Pacing (extending, focusing, extending, lifting). Note: pacing continues throughout the discussion as the group is sampled. (Watch for the children's nonverbal orienting reactions)
Reinforcement (Subconcepts)	
How do you feel about it? Which problem would you like to discuss next?	Child autonomy (feeling tone)

What did it do for you? It sounds to me like you under-stand; do you? Can you give more examples?	Feedback practice
What did you learn? How can we evaluate? What did you get out of it? Where does this take us? What might be the next step?	Direction and reward
Can you sum up for us?	Summary

Transfer
(Subconcepts)

Let's look for ways we can use what we talked about. What could you tell an absent class-mate about this discussion? How could you use this some-place else? At another time? How many of you found a chance to . . . ?	Set for transfer
What did you understand?	Meaningfulness
How was this like . . . ? What might be the same?	Similar elements
Could you also try? Outside of this class would you . . . ?	New instances

The major divisions of the questioning approach are (1) readi-ness, (2) reinforcement, and (3) transfer. Clusters of concepts within each area have a progressive, cumulative, and dependent relationship. Thus the assumption is that as the first major cluster is in operation, the second has the possibility of functioning, and, when the first and second are in action, the third becomes pos-sible. Figure 15 displays these concepts in the teaching-learning approach just illustrated with the sample questions.

Taped class discussions can be coded for questions aimed at these types of concepts in a teaching-learning approach designed to promote creative, interactive listening. Sample coding sheets are shown in Figures 16 and 17. Inaccurate listening was consid-ered a supporting variable to be accounted for in creative problem solving.

Perhaps the material in this section should be in the chapter on techniques of teaching listening. But there is much about testing that is inseparable, fortunately, from instruction. Probably the most productive testing is that which is also instructional.

Affective Response

Terms such as *aesthetic appreciation, emotional response,* and *empathy* found in some of the suggested skills in chapter three suggest areas of communicable experience that are difficult to explore by quantifiable test responses. Laughter, tears, and signs of embarrassment may give better evidence of listening than any objective test yet designed. But such evidence is colored by the listener's control of her or his expression and the power and the bias of the observer. Standardized tests, nevertheless, will not satisfy the need for day-to-day assessment, especially of long-range effects and specific requirements of a particular individual or group that needs exposure to a wide variety of dialects and usage.

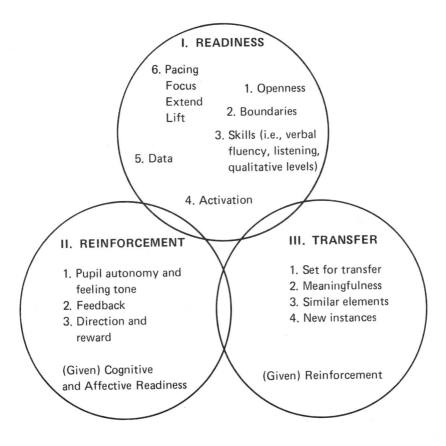

Fig. 15. Teacher questioning of students can promote the development of certain interdependent concepts.

Coding Sheet for Teacher Behavior

Teacher #_____ Teacher Functions	Teacher Responses								
	Facts, Conditions	Grouping	Labeling	Missing Data	Search Strategy	Main Problem	Type of Problem	Hypotheses	Total
Readiness									
Openness									
Boundaries									
Subskills									
Focusing on f & c									
Refocusing									
Extending									
Lifting									
Reinforcement									
Direction and reward									
Summarizing									
Transfer									
Set									
Meaning									
Similar elements									
New instances									
Other									
Control									
Unclassifiable									
Total									

Fig. 16. The teacher's ability to ask effective questions can be enhanced by coding taped samples of class discussion.

Coding Sheet for Student Behavior

Class #_____ Student Responses	Student #									
	1	2	3	4	5	6	7	8	9	Totals
Total number of responses										
Qualities Interactions										
Controlled and unclassifiable										
Concrete response										
Abstract response										
Mixed concrete and abstract										
Inaccurate listening										
Hierarchy of Qualities Elaboration										
Originality										
Multiple alternatives										
Empathy										
Causal thinking										
Tentative causal thinking										
Evaluation										
Autonomy										
Total Quality										
Creative Problem Solving Facts and conditions										
Grouping f & c										
Labeling f & c										
Missing data										
Search strategy										
Main problem										
Type of problem										
Hypotheses										
Other Regress										
Leap										

Fig. 17. Analysis of pupil responses is also necessary for refinement of teacher questions that promote creative thinking.

Summary, Cautions, and New Directions

Actually, the teacher who asks a child to repeat last-minute instructions is administering an informal listening test, with results
that may have predictive value for similar encounters. Supervisors
who adjust their speech according to their estimates of the listener's ability to interpret it estimate ability to comprehend
spoken language. Principals are testing listening when they adopt
one level of talk for a child of six and another for a child of
twelve. But in each of these instances, the immediate if not the
only interest of the "tester" is not to estimate general listening
ability, but to estimate grasp and retention of specific information.
Two classic studies suggest that the average teacher's unaided
assessment of the listening ability of individual children, even after
months of opportunity for observing, is highly unreliable (Brown,
1954; Caffrey, 1953). Both informal and formal means of assessment have a place.

What about Motivation and Testing?

In spite of the advantages of standardized, norm-referenced tests,
many paper-pencil types of evaluations lack intrinsic motivation.
They may provide little or no opportunity for a child to see the
actual consequences of how he or she listens. Children need to see
the direct cause-effect relations (important to *them*) that are the
product of the quality of their listening.

For example, can children see that they are missing out on
listening fun, beauty, and joy? ("That makes my ears happy!"
said one kindergartner.) Can children see that when they garbled
the directions, the game was spoiled? Can children see that friend-
ships bloom during empathetic listening and shrivel during one-
sided communication? Can they see that the smooth-voiced TV
announcer talked them into spending all their hard-earned allow-
ance on a stupid, flimsy toy when a little critical listening could
have saved them this disappointment? These are the real-life
evaluations that the constructors of paper-pencil tests find hard
to simulate.

If children recognize their problems in listening as their own
challenges to be overcome creatively, much of the struggle is won.
When children see that the paper and pencil tests give them
information that helps to solve their problems, learning is enhanced. It is doubtful, however, that this autonomous, creative
problem-solving emphasis can be activated by the published

directions in a manual. Long-term development of this crucial learning set rests with the teacher and her or his instructional materials. Efficient listening skills are the reward of the students who make it their personal challenge to maintain such skills at a high level. The degree of attention that listeners give reflects the extent to which they feel involved.

A last comment on research in testing listening: Is scientism in operation when researchers ask questions about listening? Progress in the listening area has not been great, for it appears to come from a rethinking of basics, not from refinements. A sound theory of the total or large listening-communicating process probably cannot be obtained by looking at some limited part of it. Straight-line models of communication are not adequate. They run something like this: A ( ) B = X, in which a communicator, A, "communicates" something in some manner via some channel, ( ), to a receiver, B, with the result or consequence X. There are sophisticated refinements of this model, but it is still a narrow conception that may be holding back progress (Thayer, 1968).

For example, listening to *I love you* brings a reaction not nearly so dependent upon *how* it is said as *when.* Success or failure of intercommunication depends not upon knowledge content, but upon the changing state of the relationship between the people involved. Crucial variables are often in the surrounding conditions of an encounter—conditions coming out of a complex and unpredictable sequence of happenings, irreversible, not fully controllable. There is a continuum of outcomes, from inevitable to possible, serendipitous, and essentially impossible. Presumably the last two, being unique and unreplicable, cannot be approached in terms of cause and effect or probability. But the important variable may not be certainty, but the very uncertainty or unpredictable variability. Thus the question: Is current science appropriate to any or all of the most important questions about listening?

At present, the state of the art of evaluating listening seems to be best described by these terms: relatively scarce, reasonably reliable, but often confused; lacking in imagination, but becoming more widespread, with a greater range; and continuing to attract interest.

5 What Are Listening Materials and Teaching-Learning Roles?

The purpose of the last chapter was to investigate listening tests; this chapter sets standards and reviews some of the materials and hardware available to assist teachers in reaching their objectives. It also concentrates on teaching strategies and role behaviors for both teachers and children. These are then integrated into a framework that is useful as a large category checklist for observing behavior that a teacher models and pupils emulate. The framework answers questions about the where, what, why, and how of listening instruction.

What Materials Are Available for Classroom Use?

At present, a large part of teaching is devoted to overcoming the damage done by totally ineffective instructional materials (Markel, 1973). As school people increasingly apply validated standards to educational products, the quality of material will improve. Teachers need to be alerted to reasons for selecting materials, reasons that depend on the purpose of lesson sequences and on how teachers view learning processes. For example, why and when does a teacher present workbook discrimination tasks as opposed to imaginative play with stories and words? Part of the task is substantiating the value of objectives and selecting a curriculum geared to the specific needs of students. As know-how for product "engineering" becomes more relevant to the classroom, it is hoped that better materials and information will be offered to users. In general, materials range from single, isolated recordings to attempts at careful, rigorous, sequential product development. When you examine materials, you might ask such questions as these:[1]

1. *Significance.* Does the material deal with significant or worthwhile behavior? Is it important to children? (If not, no matter how attractive it might look—even if it's free— forget it.)

2. *Rationale.* Does the description of the material give the basis for the theoretical, developmental, or experimental rationale? What definitions of learner, learning, content, etc., are explicit or implicit? What assumptions are made? What inferences can be made? What goals are projected?

3. *Adequacy of information for users.* Does the description tell me what I need to know about the group for which it is designed and the conditions under which it will be used? (For example, are my children at the developmental level they would need to be to use the material, or is the material too abstract? Will I need aides and specific equipment?)

4. *Product testing.* Does the publisher give me any genuine evidence of the effectiveness of the material (such as try-outs) and when, on whom, and with what results? Is there any built-in evaluation?

5. *Flexibility and opportunity for user creativity.* Does the material lend itself to modification so that I can adapt it specifically, add my own creative touch, and let the children add theirs? (That is, does it stimulate creativity and meet individual needs?)

6. *Practicality.* Is the material feasible for me in my situation? (For example, is it not only suitable for my children, but is the product easy to handle and to operate; is it packaged durably as well as appealingly; is it designed to prevent accidental erasure; will it fit standard hardware; and does it have replaceable components if they are needed?)

7. *Content.* Does the content represent a varied, challenging, appropriate, even artistic diet? What of the vocabulary? Will the material excite? What uses of language does it demonstrate: self-expression, exposition, literature, persuasion?

8. *Acoustic standards.* Does the product meet acceptable media standards? Is the voice clear and well modulated; does it capture the necessary sound frequencies?

9. *Better to do it yourself (and save your money).* Does the material represent something that I am just as well off, or better off, constructing myself—if I can find the time and resources?

What Are Some Sample Programs?

The next section presents a sample of ambitious listening programs available for the elementary and junior high levels. Your examination of them in light of the evaluative standards just given is recommended. It is well to know what is available and to build your own program by "standing on the shoulders" of others.

Historically, after the round of studies researching the amount of time spent in listening came a round of research studies, which is still in progress, designed to give evidence that planned instruction results in improved listening abilities. One researcher states that, although there have been apparently successful attempts to teach certain kinds of listening behavior, in view of the uncertainty about what listening tests measure, it is difficult to decide exactly what kinds of competencies or performances are being improved in these experiments. Since basic linguistic competence in grammar and vocabulary is probably susceptible to improvement only over long periods of time and with much effort, it is probable that teaching listening is mainly a matter of training that leads children to pay more attention to what they hear and to organize meanings for better retention, comparison, and inference (Carroll, 1968).

Listen and Read and *Listen and Think* are two excellent programs available from the Educational Developmental Laboratories. The *Listen and Read* program offers graded instructional materials for intermediate, junior high, and senior high levels. Taped lessons are self-contained and auto-instructional. The narrator introduces a skill and gives illustrations. The student is then directed to workbook exercises; the tape narrator gives the correct responses. The main emphasis is on reading and listening to instructions. *Listen and Think* extends from beginning through twelfth-grade reading levels. There are fifteen tape recordings, one skill to each tape, with an accompanying student book that contains sections to be read, some key words defined pictorially, and some dictionary-type definitions. The skills are classified as (1) analytical, (2) interpretive, (3) appreciative, and (4) critical. Total time for the recording and exercise ranges from thirty to forty-five minutes. One portion of the lesson includes a quite moderate increase in speed as levels advance called "speeded listening." The child is informed of the skill to be practiced. The lesson concludes with a short summary of what was learned.[2] Progress is charted, and graphed.

The teacher's handbook suggests follow-up activities for each lesson and gives suggestions for transfer to other subject areas. EDL has also furnished reports of investigations on the effectiveness of their materials, which provide practice in a wide range of thinking skills. Later tapes depend on earlier tapes for proper skill development.

Reading Improvement through Auditory Perceptual Training,
the result of a three-year Title III project, is a set of listening
materials directed especially toward reading improvement. This
field-tested series of four self-contained units of thirty-nine tape-
recorded lessons (averaging nine to fifteen minutes) contains
student listening booklets and teachers' manuals—all dealing with
auditory perception. The program is designed to improve the
reading achievement of elementary school children who are below
the mean for their chronological age, who fail to pay attention,
who are easily distracted by classroom noise, or who have trouble
with sound differences and with understanding and remembering
what they hear. The materials include diagnostic and review tests.

The perceptual training lessons include identification and discrimination of musical and speech sounds, short- and long-term
memory tasks, time sequencing, use of figure-ground discrimination of competing messages, auditory closure tasks, auditory
synthesis, analysis, intonation patterns, subject-verb agreement,
active and passive voice, and syntax. Materials for use in grades 1
to 3 and in learning disability groups through grade 6 were field
tested on more than 1,500 children.[3]

The following tests have been administered individually to 300
children in the project: Peabody Picture Vocabulary, Digit Span
(WISC), Northwestern Syntax Screening Test, Auditory and
Sound Blending (Illinois Test of Psycholinguistic Abilities),
Anderson-Metraux Test for Auditory Memory Span, Van Riper
Synthesis and Analysis Test, Gilmore Oral Reading Test, Boston
Speech-Sound Discrimination Test, Visual-Aural Digit Span Test
by Koppitz, and one group-administered test—Competing Messages, an auditory screening test by Hedrick and Manning (described in the preceding chapter). Data from this project should
make it possible to determine more precisely the kinds of auditory
perceptual training that are needed for children with different
learning and developmental characteristics.

Sound, Order, Sense (SOS), published by Follett, is a two-year
program in auditory perception that teaches the interrelationships
among sounds that make up speech, the sequence of sounds in
words and words in groups, and the attributes that give meaning to
words. Level one is used in first grade and level two after level one
has been completed or for older children who have auditory
perceptual difficulties. Materials can be used with an entire class or
with groups or individuals. Suggested time is approximately
twenty minutes per day.

A teacher's guide, a pupil-response book with invisible ink for immediate feedback, and simple shapes and designs instead of culturally biased and distracting pictures are included, as are 160 activity cards, follow-up suggestions for the teacher, and 11 records. One record in each level is of environmental sounds. Records are used with the "sound" tasks in the Pupil Response Books every fifth day to provide background noise against which the children listen to sentences repeated by the teacher. Other recordings provide practice for discriminating sequence, fast and slow, loud and soft, one sound and more than one, near and far, long and short, and up and down. Recordings use speech, music, environmental sounds, or a combination (but not competing speech). The teacher's guide has four well-written informative chapters on listening. No information is given at this point on tryouts. Examine this program and others in light of the criterion of interest level of the content.

The Kindergarten Auditory Screening Test, also published by Follett, complements this instructional program. By means of a record, the test measures: (1) listening to discriminate against noise (figure-ground), (2) synthesizing phonemes into words; and (3) telling whether or not paired words are the same. The figure-ground portions appear rather easy, unless the child is hard of hearing or brain damaged.

The Listening Skills Program (Science Research Associates) extends from the primary grades through the intermediate level. There are six units, one for each of the first six grades, with two cassette tapes for each level that contain twenty-four lessons for each grade (it is also available in reel-to-reel and on records). Some of the topics covered at the primary level are awareness of pitch and volume, following directions, developing sentence patterns, conceptualizing that sound implies action, awareness of fantasy, and using context to develop vocabulary. Some of the topics at the intermediate level are auditory discrimination, instant recall, following directions, remembering sequence, listening for cause and effect, visualizing and listening for mood information, and distinguishing fact and opinion.

Auditory Perception Training is a series that can be used for students who have minimal brain dysfunction, those who have auditory perception deficits, and those in a school developmental readiness program. It can be used with small groups or with classes. The program has five areas of three levels each: (1) Auditory Memory (following directions), (2) Auditory Imagery (visualizing and selecting a picture described), (3) Auditory Figure-Ground (following one of two competing messages), (4) Auditory Motor (drawing lines according to directions), and (5) Auditory Discrimination (marking a picture that goes with a nonverbal or verbal sound). There are mimeographed student worksheets, teachers' editions, tape cassettes, and a chart that identifies concepts and materials that are prerequisite to a lesson. Examples are color recognition (red, yellow); directional awareness (around, on, above); and shape and figure recognition (canoe, cupcake, mask, tandem, umbrella, square). Tryout data were not included. Material in the Auditory Figure-Ground subtests may not be sufficiently varied or controlled in the area of signal-to-distraction ratio, i.e., does the distraction really interfere? Moreover, fifteen seconds response time seems a bit long.

Instructional sequences for auditory discrimination are seldom based on developmental or experimental research. Teaching comes mainly from the folklore of past individual successes and common sense about moving from what is easiest for children to hear to what appears to be more difficult and less consistent.

A rare example of a developmentally oriented program is the Auditory Discrimination Skills component of the Perceptual Skills Curriculum, developed by the University of Pittsburgh's Research and Development Center. The improved skills appear to help children read lists of words. Presented in detail, the program illustrates the current analysis of teacher-learner behavior that lends itself to "accountability." The concluding paragraphs of this section give cautions and reservations about such a program.

The Pittsburgh program is based on two developmental ideas. The first might be tagged "global to differentiated" and the second "decrease in the need for bodily movement to accompany information processing." The "global to differentiated" idea pertains to the acquisition of skills as the child progresses from large, global wholes to refined and eventually interrelated parts. For example, Tom plays with whole words and then is able to isolate, repeat, and move about a single sound within a word—if he needs to. But then, although Tom has developed to the point of being able to differentiate if he wants to, he also needs to progress to the point of being able to bypass minute analysis economically. An analogy is found in the person learning to drive a car. The learner has a global idea of the action involved and can break down the task into separate actions, but later can avoid spending energy on consciously attending to each separate maneuver in, say, shifting and signaling.

The second developmental idea, "decrease in bodily movement needed to accompany information processing," pertains to the child's ability to analyze and arrange sounds in proper sequence with less and less dependence on touch, grasping, and vocal-muscular cues. For example, the child can move from clapping out musical rhythms to symbolizing with dashes to efficiently and simply holding patterns of sound in memory with little conscious effort.

One year olds analyze their visual world more reliably if they can accompany what they see with some bodily contact. Later they behave as if imaginary hands extended from their eyes. There still may be a motor part to their behavior, but it is less obvious. Until children learn to look at symbols representing what they have heard, speaking aloud is a reliable method for exploring what they have listened to. For example, Jane might be overheard repeating to herself, "autobile, aumobile, automobile." This overt behavior declines in frequency as she matures, as her patterns of sound become familiar, as she becomes more efficient and apparently analyzes sound only down to the level she needs for swift use (Rosner, 1972).

A description of specific child behaviors in the Pittsburgh program follows. In general, the teaching distinguishes three levels: Level 1, global, nonverbal, bodily movement; Level 2, verbal syllables and movement; Level 3, embedded language sound discriminated and produced.

Level 1

The children march and clap hands in time to recorded music. (Rhythm organizes time. Sounds produced in time group more easily and more meaningfully with rhythm. Younger, less-developed listeners need such structures to help them order sound in time.)

In the next step, the children clap hands once for each word in a spoken phrase of single-syllable words, as in "a big blue ball."

Then they draw horizontal dashes from left to right, substituting each dash for a clap.

They "read" the dashes in any requested order.

Some children, of course, do not need to start at this level of the program; observational testing quickly shows the teacher that higher levels, or no basic skills program at all, are appropriate for a particular learner.

Level 2

Children clap to, make, and "read" dashes for two- and three-syllable words, as in $\left\{\begin{array}{c}\text{croc-o-dile}\\ \underline{}\ \underline{}\ \underline{}\end{array}\right\}$, to indicate parts of words. The child responds by moving from words of one syllable to those of more than one syllable.

Level 3

The children speak an omitted sound when they are given a spoken word followed by a restatement of it with consonant sound omitted, e.g., "Say *meat.* Now say *eat.* What sound was left out the second time?" "Say *belt.* Now say *bell.* What sound was left out that second time?"

In essence, once the children have mastered the ability to "read" dashes, the teacher exposes them to the concepts of sounds embedded in a phrase or word. They first note the syllable, then even smaller units of sound at the beginning, in the middle, and at the end of words and finally in consonant blends, e.g., /k/ in *make;* /w/ in *s(w)ing (sing).*

In the higher levels of the program, the child demonstrates skill by deleting portions of words and voicing others. For example, shown side-by-side the pictures of a cow and a boy, the child is told: "Say *cow.* Say *boy.*" Then the picture of the boy is covered and the child is asked to "say it again, but don't say *boy.* Say *picnic* without *pic, man* without the *m, block* without the *b*" (quite a fine discrimination).

Ideally, a child will have a reliable listener to help him or her respond during this program. But to help the busy, unassisted instructor who has forty children to teach, there are story materials, recordings, and "write and see" answer sheets that turn color when the child marks the appropriate space.

Use of the above program can highlight certain listening skills that are often neglected in ordinary teaching units. Of course, some children do, incidentally, receive through their school experience enough practice in auditory discrimination, as, for example, when they participate in a literature program that is accompanied by oral language and composition. Still other children learn listening skills in classroom activities like those below.

Meow's new name. A simple, productive device for a quick probe of a child's grasp of sound-letter correspondences for consonants is an attractive picture of a cat with its name visible and a slot for first-letter substitution(s) to be made. Say: "This cat's name is *Meow*. He gets tired of his name and wants a new name. When I take away the first letter of his name and put in a new letter, say his new name that begins with that letter and rhymes with *Meow*." Use, for example, *Seow, Beow, Deow, Bleow*. This will quickly provide information on sound identification and capital letter recognition. Use of small *d*'s and *b*'s may reveal a lack of letter discrimination rather than sound discrimination.) You can also obtain information on the use of blends and the grasp of the concept of rhyming in about a minute. You can vary the pictorial device according to age and cultural interests, and you don't need expensive testing materials. (Thanks to Jane Root, who uses a clown named Bojo, for this idea.)

Name game. Auditory discrimination activities for beginners frequently include guided inductive approaches, during which the teacher begins to develop the concept of "sound alike." Calling attention to lips and sounds, the teacher repeats the names of children in the class, such as *Mary, Michael,* and *Martha.* Next, the teacher contrasts these names with a name such as *Jerry* and later with a "closer-in" example such as *Nancy.* Then the teacher asks the children to produce their own examples of names or words that begin with the same sound as *Mary* and those that do not. Once auditory discrimination develops to some extent, the teacher can combine the sound with the written letter. If the child actually forms or writes the letter, it may help him or her in attaining and reinforcing the concept of "sound alike—look alike." Some teachers make a game of letting children get their coats (or other dismissal activities) on the basis of the sounds in their names: "If your name begins like *lollipop,* you may go."

Object sorting by sound. Have the children sort unlabeled objects or pictures into categories of names that begin with the same sound. The child can then name other objects that belong in the group. The objects (such as button, box, ball, marble, money, mirror, pencil, pen, pin, etc.) are named verbally at first. As a variation that will add interest, hide the objects in a grab bag. The child draws out an item, says its name, and gets to "keep" it if he or she can say another word that begins or ends with the same sound.

How Can the Teacher Use Trade Books?

Children's literature published as trade books is highly motivational for developing listening skills that range from perception of sound (acuity) to discrimination between sounds to comprehension of what the sounds mean. Generally speaking, children have heard language used in many ways: in day-to-day transactions, in self-expressive epithets, in scientific discourse, and in persuasive discourse. But children may not have had much chance to listen to the literary use of language. What a loss! Books are excellent vehicles for developing listening skills, in addition to their many other values, and children will listen to them closely. But how? What are some of the specific teaching strategies and books that develop listening skills?

Listening games are a natural outgrowth of the reading of such books as May Garelick's *Sounds of a Summer Night* (Addison-Wesley) or Paul Showers' *The Listening Walk* (Crowell). Children listen for or make the sounds they hear in the stories. Children need to listen for sound sequence to get the fun out of Pat Hutchins's *The Surprise Party* (Macmillan) and *Don't Forget the Bacon* (Greenwillow). Some young children adore cumulative tales and develop skills associated with learning the sequence of events. One of the most popular such books is Paul Galdone's *The House That Jack Built* (McGraw-Hill). Other favorites are Nonny Hogrogian's *One Fine Day* (McGraw-Hill) and Galdone's *The Gingerbread Boy* (Seabury). In *One Fine Day* the fox, who wants his tail sewn back in place, repeats the sequence of events at each stop in this tale. The old game of gossip illustrates how messages passed along become garbled, with amusing or disastrous results. Similarly, in Doris Orgel's *The Uproar* (McGraw-Hill) a child thinks his mother said she was going to the *uproar* rather than to the *opera.*

Discriminating among sounds is a spontaneous response to other books. Peter Spier's *Crash, Bang, Boom* and *Gobble, Growl, Grunt* (both Doubleday) use sounds as a means of identification. Both books invite children to join in and to distinguish among the sounds heard. Florence P. Heide's *Sound of Sunshine, Sound of Rain* (Parents) portrays a blind boy's use of sound to find a friend. Margaret Wise Brown's Noisy Book series (Harper) calls attention to the variety of sounds heard in different locales. Byrd Baylor's *Plink, Plink, Plink* (Houghton) speculates on what sounds seem like at night, and Helen Borten's *Do You Hear What I Hear?* (Abelard-Schuman) increases attentiveness to various sounds.

Books can help to develop higher levels of listening comprehension. For example, Charlotte Steiner's *Listen to My Seashell* (Knopf) explores the concept of sound. Lois Kaufman's *What's That Noise?* (Lothrop) encourages children to think productively about new and frightening experiences. Roger Duvoisin's *Petunia,*

I Love You (Knopf) builds on inferences and hypothesizing about outcomes. When Racoon tries to trap Petunia so that he can eat her, concerned listeners will want to warn her. Arnold Lobel's *Owl at Home* (Harper), an easy-to-read book, encourages even very young children to make inferences about the bumps in Owl's bed and why his tear-water tea tastes salty.

In essence, children learn many listening skills during story time without detracting from the primary objective of enjoying a good story. An important motivational plus for both teacher and child is the beauty, artistry, and sheer visual pleasure offered by fine children's literature.

Follett has a collection of Junior Listen-Hear books for pre-school through grade one and a package for grades one-three; examples are the *Silly Listening Book* and *An Ear Is to Hear.* Included are detailed Teachers' Source Books with guidelines for auditory discrimination and listening exercises. *Sound Science* (Prentice Hall), for children four to eight, answers questions about the nature of sound with the help of an engaging cartoon figure, a Gloop, who helps children to work like a scientist.

The child who becomes interested in sound, not only in relation to his or her own listening, but in the broader context of science, can find it intriguing to compare *Sound and Ultrasonics* by Adler, written in 1959, with *Sounds You Cannot Hear* by Windle. The latter discusses the application of ultrasonics in medicine and in industry (ages eight-eleven). Children are often enticed by listening instruction material that feeds out of or into appealing science or social science areas. See also Gene Liberty's *The First Book of the Human Senses* (F. Watts).

Middle Grades

Examples of techniques and materials for the middle grades include the Houston-created program for a fourth-grade group of culturally deprived children that contains suggestions for the teacher on direction giving, questioning, give-and-take in conversation, and understanding nonverbal ways of communicating.

A study done in Sweden of 550 pupils ten, eleven, and twelve years old is designed to interrelate listening, reading, speaking, and writing. Among the materials are tape cassettes and booklets (contact Göran Strömqvist, Director, Teachers College, 431 20 Mölndal, Sweden).

The listening materials and program for the Thinking Improvement Project designed for about the fifth-grade level have been cited earlier (Lundsteen, 1969a and b, 1976a and b). The problem-solving program that gave much of the learning set needed in the listening program has also been described (Lundsteen, 1970a, 1976a and b).

A study at the sixth-grade level investigated the ability of pupils to use certain verbal context clues in listening and in reading (the skill Brown suggested as the single best predicting skill in general listening). The implication of this study is that boys of low reading level do better when they use listening for certain context clues that were constructed out of definitions or descriptions (Chang, 1968). To assure success, instruction might begin with this listening skill, move to reading, and then to other types of clues.

Tapp (1953) gives a description of a lesson that illustrates that fairly young children can understand rumor. It illustrates the distortion that occurs when a description of a picture is related by one child to another.

Another study (Edgar, 1961) at the fourth-, fifth-, and sixth-grade levels used four different techniques to teach listening: (1) summary (at intervals children were asked to pause three seconds and summarize to themselves); (2) analogies (the group listened to the stem of an oral analogy and then completed the analogy from a selection of four words on an answer sheet—plus listening to a series of five words); (3) vocabulary (the group listened to thirty-word paragraphs and then defined an unknown word from contextual clues that were not differentiated as to types); (4) story method (groups listened to an original story and answered true-false questions). Results were measured by an author-constructed test. After eight weeks of use, the second method appeared to be the best, but the study should be re-designed somewhat and replicated.

A teaching technique that is appropriate to all grade levels involves creative dramatics whereby both affective and cognitive thinking skills associated with listening can be developed. An NCTE/ERIC monograph is available on this topic (Hoetker, 1969). There are many treatments that use dramatization; for example, Stewig (1970) has written in an interesting manner on language growth through creative dramatics. (See also Bednarz, 1971, and Kirkton, 1971.)

High School Level

A report (Bloom, 1954), early but still applicable, contains a detailed unit consisting of criteria for the evaluation of television and radio news broadcasts. Boston University has produced a series of studies on critical listening, mainly at the high school level. One of the studies evaluated a series of fourteen recorded lessons designed to make tenth-grade pupils aware of eight propaganda techniques that were presented during a three-week course. Other studies in this series, including the pioneer work of Devine, have been reviewed elsewhere (Lundsteen, 1969a). The studies are full of ideas for materials and practical procedures (Devine, 1967, 1968, 1978; also see the work of his doctoral students, e.g., DeVito, 1977; DiBiasio, 1977. Gratz, 1973, describes three miniunits on listening presented over a three-week period).

One of the most complete descriptions of a classroom program is by Brown (1954); it presents ideas applicable to almost any grade level. He calls it "a feasible course of instruction in English which accords auding an attention commensurate with its importance." Brown suggests that, first, the teacher of English shares with other teachers a major responsibility identified by such terms as *personal adjustment, character development,* and *self-actualization.* Second, the teacher has responsibilities defined by the meaning of the word *English.* The major choice in interpreting the word *English* lies between its designation of the language we speak (linguistic needs of the pupils) and its meaning in the statement "I never liked English in school" (an established content, sanctioned by tradition). His point of view is that the task of the English teacher begins and ends with the highest possible development of skill in the native tongue—in listening, speaking, reading, and writing. Other possible English contents are justifiable only in that they help to fulfill that special task.

Next Brown outlines, for example, procedures for making initial interest and ability inventories, identification and permanent seating placement of those with known hearing loss, identification of superior listeners, individual and small-group listening conferences, daily exercises, weekly tests, a system of simplified phonemic notation, and individual vocabulary sheets. (Also see Bursuk, 1971, on listening versus reading presentation for improvement of retarded readers.)

College Level

Duker lists forty-nine studies at the college level, most of which are associated with beginning communications programs or with the effect of rhetorical devices on listeners, including an interesting project for the development of programmed materials for use in listening to public speaking in a beginning course. The goal of this linear program was the identification within contemporary speech samples of the central ideas of speech, main divisions, pattern of organization and supporting materials, motive appeals, and characteristics of language (Erway, 1967). Listening consists of preparation for listening, the listening process itself, and the post-listening period, which should emphasize immediate recall to aid retention. (See also Duker, 1970, for an evaluation of five programs used in business and industry.) Two college-level programs are mentioned by Walsh (1970) and by Cottrill and Alciatore (1974). Cottrill and Alciatore experimented with a systematic programmed approach (Xerox and a "conventional" approach).

What Hardware and Media Can Teachers Use?

An effective listening environment may involve both hardware and software that may be part of planned and constructed teaching units. *Undergirding these aids, of course, is the indispensable establishing of the climate of close, open, interpersonal communication with self-acceptance and opportunity for unpredictable creativity.* This section discusses hardware for teaching and media in general.

Television, videotape cassettes, listening centers, language masters, 16mm and 8mm films and loops, combination filmstrip-records, kits, labs, even office intercoms—all are being used to serve the teaching of listening. One school appropriated the principal's intercom and used it for giving listening lessons. Children in the first grade responded to their names being called and to specific directions (McKee, 1967).

Television was cited at the beginning of this book as affecting listening. The solution is not to turn it off, but to use its appeal for teaching purposes (Kirshner, 1969). Such programs as "Wild Kingdom," "Discovery," some family specials, the "Undersea World of Jacques Cousteau," and "CBS Children's Film Festival" are commendable. Such programs, listed in *Teacher's Guide to Television,*[4] may eventually be available on videotape cassettes to be dropped into the classroom apparatus and will provide intriguing yet guided learning. But "wonderful communication systems —but little communication" must be avoided (Ball and Bogatz, 1972).

A recommendation for the content and process of educational TV that will provide more communication: let there be challenging, discussion-provoking content, such as is found in the best of children's literature. Stop the hubbub and the bang-bang, hurry-hurry pace. Let the program wait a moment while the children talk back to the TV characters and to persons watching with them. Perhaps the program might present model children in front of their own sets responding to "What-do-you-think?" questions. Besides allowing children to "bring their experience" to the program, provide strategies for follow-up, such as "Turn off your set and go tell someone about the program . . ." "Now the next time you see a bird, you tell a friend . . . and listen . . ."

Usually a few articles are published each year on listening centers equipped with tape recorders, earphones, occasionally even cubicles and possibly a coordinated filmstrip and tape device (as in Bernthal, 1967; Gotkin and Fendiller, 1965; Helm, 1973; Schneeberg, 1977). By using tapes, children can concentrate on "school language" as distinguished possibly from their own. Original material can be created and taped by the children, sometimes by older children for younger children.

A few school districts have Dial-a-Tape systems (Reuter, 1969). For example, School District Twelve, Adams County, Colorado, has been participating in a Title III project, "To Teach—To Listen —To Learn." The district has a central collection of over 2,500 audio tapes, representing every discipline and transmitted over existing telephone lines. It can be obtained by a turn of a dial. Teachers in Adams County feel it is the next best thing to a tutor.

The Roles of the School, the Teacher, and the Pupil: A Synthesis

One appropriate synthesis of the preceding discussion in this book is to list ideas for the roles of the school, the teacher, and the pupil which can be developed from the literature of the field—and common sense. This listing invites additions, revisions, and possible deletions. Please note that many of the roles overlap and are, in fact, shared responsibilities.

Roles of the School, Its Administrator, and Its Consultants[5]

1. To view the development of all of the verbal skills—listening, speaking, reading, and writing—and their integration with one another and with thinking as the major responsibility of the elementary school.

2. To make provisions for instruction that is systematic and developmental (as well as incidental), i.e., a total school continuum of which all staff are aware.

3. To make available specific inservice training that focuses on felt needs of both new teachers, who always need help, and experienced teachers who missed learning about listening or need stimulation if only to reject the shallow comfort of routine. To provide released time for such inservice training.

4. To provide for parent education as well as teacher education by means of brochures, meetings, and classroom visits designed to present the philosophy and goals of the language program, which is so thoroughly understood and accepted by the staff that it can be communicated to laymen.

5. With staff acceptance, to provide astute decision making that is based on an appropriate combination of directives, principal-faculty discussion, and faculty decisions about the language program.

6. To provide and coordinate a program that retains what is useful in the old, selects what is valuable from the new, and actively incorporates this information by using sources such as some of those given in this book.

7. To furnish the materials, hardware, and setting for a stimulating and varied listening environment.

8. To provide for individual differences in listening.

9. To help children use their own language, whatever it is, as an effective tool.

10. To support the fulfillment of the teacher and pupil roles.

11. To provide a feedback mechanism to inform others of successes and failures of the program.

Roles of the Teacher

Ideally, as teachers acquire various desirable listening behaviors, they seek to pass them on to their students, who begin to use them. Among these desirable listening behaviors, categorized roughly, are "where," "what," "why," and "how."

Where

Teacher behaviors that deal with the environment or with climate control in the classroom are examples of "where." Other examples of observable behaviors are attempts to optimize listening channels:

1. Adjust seating to the best acoustical advantage, especially for hearing-handicapped pupils.
2. Check temperature, ventilation, appropriate degree of "quiet" (Brown, 1970), and position of the speaker in relation to the listeners.

Not only can teachers fulfill these responsibilities, but they can also guide their pupils to assume them and can reinforce with praise the success of the pupils in so doing. Some people tend to tolerate the hampering "noise" of poor environmental conditions in their listening channels, assuming that it is someone else's responsibility to correct the problem.

What

Teacher behaviors during task analysis and determination of content of listening material deal with "what." The teacher may subdivide and further break down a hierarchy of pinpointed goals, objectives, and skills until learner success is possible. Goal setting includes levels of listening performance. Also, the teacher knows "what" goes into children's information processing. A process framework of the steps and skills of a proficient listener has been described in detail in chapter two, with the help of a flowchart and a matrix of skills.

Teachers can demonstrate these skills and the process during a class discussion or in other instructional situations. They give students feedback about the skills, pointing them out and thereby reinforcing them. Children gradually learn those skills that are lifted to consciousness and associated with success.

Analyses of skills have been made by Rosner (1972) for auditory perception and discrimination in kindergarten and elementary school children and by Johnson and Friedman (1970) for other basic listening operations in children from ten to fourteen years of age—for example, children defined listening situations by selecting desired outcomes. Steps 3 through 7 elaborate teacher behavior in this category.

3. Diagnoses, selects, and appraises an appropriate sequence of of skills for individual learners.

Another dimension of "what" deals specifically with teaching procedures for using listening material and its content. Again, ideally, the teacher passes on the function of being a provider of material and an evaluator of students for their own autonomous operation.

4. Selects or develops varied listening material for specific skills and subskills at an appropriate level of difficulty and with variety.

5. Avoids ritual and the presenting of too much listening material at one time. That is, the teacher uses listening time wisely and selectively.

6. Avoids needless repetition of instructions, which encourages careless listening.

7. Helps children note what other children will listen to and appreciate.

Why

The "why," or rationale, behind teacher behavior that is committed and enthusiastic is related to the goals of listening discussed under "what." In the "why" category the teacher is prepared to explain the purpose of a listening experience, describe its importance and function, and explain why it is to the learner's advantage to listen—rather than simply demanding unquestioning obedience.

8. Knows why listening instruction is important and guides children to this realization; for example, listening as a factor in social and in economic competency is sometimes the major educational route open, especially for the disabled reader.

How

Consisting of several strategies, "how" in at least one instance is closely related to "why." This strategy is to enable learners to see reasons why they should take the trouble to learn or to practice a specific skill. Then learner motivation becomes higher; passive and active resistance diminishes. One aspect of motivation is to use advanced organizers to give a sense of direction; they may be in the form of purposes or preparation for the listening material to come.

9. Pinpoints a focus for listening.

This use of advanced organizers relates to the readiness factor in listening instruction. Here care must be taken in preparing for a new or difficult vocabulary to be used in listening material. In other words, the teacher checks the background or attained boundaries of learner performance, which includes vocabulary and other language and nonlanguage concepts.

10. Observes carefully throughout instruction for verbal and nonverbal hints of boundaries of learner performance and competence.
11. Encourages children to demand meaning for the vocabulary they hear.
12. Uses challenging vocabulary and syntax that stimulate children to reach ahead of their boundaries (Chomsky, 1972) or uses some other learning activator.

Another set of behaviors related to the "how" of instruction refers to the concept of "pacing" and its focusing, extending, and lifting strategies found in Taba (1966).

13. Calls on more than one child to respond to an open-ended question and samples layers of a group, extending facts and conditions on a more concrete level of discourse before seeking a lift in thought to a more advanced level. ("What are they before we try to group and label them?" "Tell us what you could call these, before we try to apply them to this situation or to relate them to another group.")

Another part of this "how" of pacing is simply making productive use of pauses while giving time for listening and thinking processes to operate. In other words the provocative teacher's question time is less than the pupil's answer time.

14. Uses words as concisely as possible in order to provoke responses and then waits for many responses while respecting silences.

The teacher reveals these pacing and other strategies to children by helping them acquire concepts. Concepts are acquired with inductive guidance from examples and nonexamples (Markle and Tieman, 1970, 1972).

15. For a given listening skill (generalization, strategy, or attitude), analyzes a concept and selects a rational set of examples and nonexamples that provide both crucial and irrelevant attributes for teaching and testing.

The next set of strategies pertains to reinforcement. It is suggested that during instruction in listening comprehension, learning

be strengthened by teacher behaviors that promote pupil autonomy and communicative feedback. The resulting reward comes
from a sense of direction from confirmation or satisfaction of
curiosity. Such strategies are suggested instead of candy, tokens,
points, and other extrinsic rewards.

16. Helps children achieve a sense of direction during listening
    instruction as they obtain knowledge of their apparent
    boundaries, have a chance to operate, review their perform-
    ance boundary again, and go on to a more challenging
    operation.

17. Provides feedback on results of the listening effort. ("Yes,
    that is what was communicated.") Uses outside evaluation
    to encourage self-evaluation. ("How *did* you listen?" "How
    do you listen now?")

18. Seeks feedback and encourages the seeking of feedback
    during interpersonal communication. ("What does that
    mean to you?" "Do you mean this?")

In other words, the teacher simply makes sure that pupils are told
the results of their efforts to apply their listening skills (Goolsby
and Lasco, 1970).

Besides attention to readiness of the learner, with its diagnosed
boundaries, and to the pacing strategies of focusing, extending,
and lifting and attention to reinforcement with appropriate
practice, the teacher also gives attention to the transfer of listening
skills and attitudes. The term *transfer* implies the use of retrieved
information from and about listening in a new context. Transfer
also implies the change in ability to perform as a consequence of
having completed another related listening act. The teacher fosters
this transfer by facilitating an attitude for it; making sure that the
original, reinforced learning was meaningful; helping the child to
discriminate similar aspects in the two listening contexts; providing new instances for generalized transfer; and using feedback
directed toward transfer (Lundsteen, 1968a).

19. Makes children aware that the teacher seeks the transfer of
    meaningful skills or attitudes by helping them see similar
    elements from listening situation to listening situation and
    provides new ones, with feedback, if not otherwise avail-
    able. ("What other circumstances would lead you to seek
    feedback from your listener in order to make sure he or she
    has understood you?" "Give another instance when you as a

listener would report to your speaker to make sure you heard it correctly.")

Affective Considerations

Finally, the effective teacher probably projects an attitude, value, tone, or style called empathy. This set of behaviors is probably part of the cluster for readiness, employing openness, warmth, liveliness, and sheer verbal fluency that is frequently prerequisite for genuine interpersonal communication. The teacher may simply lean forward and say warmly, "Tell me." Thus she or he is not "too much a teacher" with grim diagnostic, prescriptive determination. The use of empathy is related to the studies of role-taking in elementary school children conducted by Flavel and others (1968). In these investigations the assumption was that the ability to consider in advance the questions and informational demands of the listener (and the listener's ability to assume the role of the speaker) plays an important part in exchanging information between the two. This construct is sometimes referred to as the empathy-effective communication hypothesis (Hogan and Henly, 1970). More importantly, when children are listened to simply and warmly, it "creates" them, makes them unfold and expand. This type of affective behavior should be continued throughout the instructional components of readiness, reinforcement, and transfer.

20. Listens to children without her or his mind pressing against the children's and without arguing or changing the subject.
21. Distinguishes role attributes of the pupil; puts him or herself emotionally (as well as cognitively) in the place of the student speaker and listener. Shares responsibility for communication.

The effective teacher also considers the affective, emotional interference and personal problems of the learners as partially determining their learning boundaries. He or she exhibits affective consideration. For example, the teacher does not "chew out" a pupil and then expect that pupil to listen at her or his highest level.

These teacher behaviors that pertain to methods of readiness, reinforcement, and transfers are illustrated with the sample questions for the teacher in chapter four. In conclusion, Figure 18 summarizes the categories covered in this section on teacher behavior during listening instruction. These categories may also suggest future research possibilities.

The following is a summary checklist for teachers:

What kinds of listening do I do myself?

Do I talk too much in school or do I listen more than I talk? (Observe frequencies.)

Do I encourage the children to speak more than a single word or thought in response to a question?

Do I ensure that my choice of words does not present an impossible hurdle to the child?

But do I, on occasion, also use words that stretch listening and do I then encourage the child to demand and get meaning? (Develop a log or card system for pupils to keep.)

Are my questions so thought-provoking that my question time is less than pupil answer time?

Do children in my class follow each other spontaneously and independently without directing each comment to me, and do they react to peers as well as to adults? (Analyze changes in technique and impact according to taped sequences.)

When I give oral directions, do I prepare the pupils for what is to come and then avoid repetition? Are the directions worth hearing?

Are my directions ambiguous? (When children fail to follow directions, it may be they are avoiding an ambiguous situation.)

Is the purpose of each activity understood by each child? (Lack of pupil comprehension may result from a lack of defined purpose on the part of the teacher.)

Do I relate good listening habits to all classroom activities; is the classroom environment favorable?

Do I give the poor reader but good listener an opportunity to excel through the testing of material presented orally?

Do I enhance the child's comprehension by providing organization of the spoken material (e.g., a preview, an opportunity for pupils to relate their own past experience to the purposes of the materials)?

Whenever possible do I take time to be a "listening teacher," empathetic, ready to simply lean forward and say, "Tell me . . ."? Do I give my full attention and expect the child to begin speaking, then show constant interest, or do I reflect feeling in the manner of a clear mirror?

For an interesting study of the effectiveness of communication among third-grade pupils used as tutors, teachers, and teacher aides, see Stiggins and others (1971); also see Stammer (1977) and teacher-training research by Lundgren and Shavelson (1974).

Roles of the Pupils

Some of the following suggestions are clearly for older pupils, but almost all of them can be handled well in some form by children in the primary grades. Autonomy gives them a sense of commitment to their schooling. Maybe McLuhan is right when he says that today's children need a role before a goal. Specifically, they need:

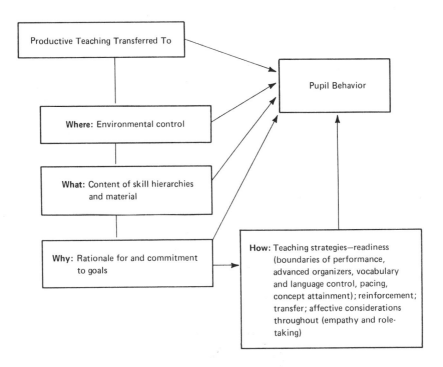

Fig. 18. A framework for productive teaching behavior during listening instruction.

1. To learn to use the listening environment more effectively.
   a. To know optimal physical listening conditions.
   b. To discover, verify, experiment with, and do research on their listening and hearing.
   c. To learn to do something about what they hear.
      (1) To be aware of different levels of listening and noise.
      (2) To be aware of different purposes of listening.
      (3) To formulate standards of good listening in various situations.
      (4) To improve their understanding of the listening process.
      (5) To learn to fix, and keep, attention on what they wish to hear.
      (6) To learn what other children will listen to.
      (7) To learn to locate and use listening material.
      (8) To learn to ask questions when in doubt about meaning.
      (9) To share with the sender the responsibility for communication.
      (10) To learn to use listening time wisely, to be selective, for example, in TV viewing.
      (11) To be responsible for self-evaluation of listening, understandings, abilities, skills, appreciations.
      (12) To exploit (to their advantage) the rate differential between thought and speech.
   d. To learn to solve personal problems the child is encountering now and will encounter in the future, partly through understanding how the listening process of "meeting of minds" can help.
2. To develop a sense of responsibility and concern for communication in the local community.
   a. To realize the importance of listening.
   b. To understand the relationship of listening to economic competency.
3. To begin to understand something of her or his cultural heritage in communication and its relationship to the present and the future.
4. To help plan, revise, and administer the program.
5. To help select, gather, and distribute supplies and materials.
6. To help identify those pupils in need of special help and those able to provide that help.

7. To help lead discussions, conduct interviews, tutor, and counsel.

8. To help to develop and maintain a high level of morale, rapport, and control.

9. To help to receive, consider, and act upon suggestions and complaints.

10. To help in selecting, constructing, administering, scoring, and evaluating pupil-formulated tests or other means of self-assessment.

11. To help evaluate performance and progress (keeping track of success has motivational value).

12. Generally, to help make decisions on "what" (materials, activities), "why" (objectives), "how" (procedures), "when" (setting up the schedules), "who" (people on what committees), "where" (in the neighboring classroom, library, auditorium), and "how well" (evaluative procedures).

Individual Differences

Children have individual differences in learning through listening. Some pupils learn rapidly by listening, some slowly, some in fits and spurts, some in hunks, lumps, or wholes. Some can listen for a long time; others need to turn to other activities. Some can sit down with a tape and earphones and get much out of listening on their own. Some require a breakdown of listening into specific steps, together with a lot of guidance, and some need distinct cues from without. Some children process information more quickly than others because they know just where to attend. Some must take it more slowly. Some fast assimilators can cope with a great deal of new material. Others are troubled by new information; each new listening task is quite a chore. Some need to assimilate the entire listening unit; they cannot take in further information until every aspect of the previous information has been thought about and followed thoroughly. Others listen much more impulsively and impatiently. They want to go ahead without being sure that they know what has gone before. They may be so eager for what lies ahead that they have not adequately grasped all of the earlier message. The teacher's role is to use listening material in ways that make the most sense to each child within his or her present way of learning and style of assimilation, insofar as they can be determined.

Further Research Is Still Needed

In the Duker annotated bibliography (1968) there are at least eighteen entries dealing with needed research. Suggestions have also been made throughout this book; many more are probably now apparent to the reader. A few additional areas that might be studied are the personality adjustment dimension of listening, utilization of compressed (and expanded) speech, growth patterns, skills—how to teach them and with what material, and listening vocabulary, such as in the excellent, early (1951) study by Weir, in Duker (1968).

Existing studies might be replicated and future studies devised with more specific criteria, such as detailed reports of how the teacher is actually behaving, how the pupil is actually behaving, and what the interaction is. Evidence that would verify these behaviors might be obtained, for example, from videotape, observation scales administered by trained personnel (including both verbal and nonverbal behaviors), or stenographic records. Collection of such evidence and placement in a data bank would allow investigators to make additional use of the data, according to recommendations by the Cooperative Research Committee of the National Conference on Research in English.

Epilogue

There is a children's poem that may have a message for educators as well:

> Some say that owls are wise
> Because they keep so quiet.
> Could most of us fare better
> On an expert listening diet?

What is an "expert listening diet"? These chapters have made many suggestions, in addition to pointing out the impact of listening on reading and the other language arts. But one point should be stressed: to quote Emerson, "Be not too much a teacher."

There may be a grim determination to "make the children listen." Some educators adopt the "professional thesis": a child is best treated as an object; helping the child is based on expertise; the expert advises, manipulates, and molds the child to produce the desired result. Some educators realize that our world is ruled in part by those at the conference table who are capable of skillful thought and expression derived from skilled listening. A grim diagnostic-prescriptive determination is understandable. Educators foresee rapid change in new curricula and content, new possibilities in multimedia, educational technology, and accountability— and diagnostic-prescriptive instruction in and through listening seems appropriate. But these conscientious educators must also sense dangers in the programs that stress passive skills in passive listening. In addition to hindering the development of autonomous persons, other dangers stem from ignoring the factors of fatigue, personal problems, emotional interference, and the child's need for casual argument with peers.

When listening instruction focuses on a creative problem-solving climate, children are less likely to get lost personally. Part of this climate is that others listen to them. When this happens, it "creates them"; it helps them unfold and expand. When children are listened to, ideas begin to grow within them, and they come to life and are then happier and freer. When teachers and children listen to one another, an alternating current emerges, recharging both. Continually recreated, they rarely tire of one another.

In essence, tell yourself to listen with affection to children who talk to you. Try to know them without your mind pressing against theirs or arguing or changing the subject. If Mary's talk seems a little meager just now, remind yourself that "presently, she will come alive." Desire to know how children feel and want them to know how you feel. If educators cannot communicate, they become lost, too.

Appendixes

Appendix A
Commercially Published
Listening Materials

Aardvark and Imperial International; Bob Puig, Representative; 523 North Hanover, Anaheim, CA 92801, (714) 827-5708
Auditory Discrimination Program; Gateway to Good Reading

Bowmar Publishing Company, 622 Rodier Drive, Glendale, CA 91201
Bowmar Language Communication Program; Multi-Media Reading Incentive Program

Developmental Learning Materials; Susan W. Noble, Representative; 4137 Mendez Street, Long Beach, CA 90815, (213) 498-1500
Auditory Perception Training (APT); Concepts for Communication (CFC)

Disney Records and Books; Chapman Distributing Company; Al Chapman, Representative; 1212 South Albany Street, Los Angeles, CA 90015, (213) 749-9484
Reading-along books with record; The Story Teller Series; Disneyland Story Tapes

Economy Company, PO Box 25308, 1901 North Walnut, Oklahoma City, OK 73125
Pacer; Sounds and Stories

Educational Activities, Inc., Box 392, Freeport, NY 11520
Basic Elementary Spelling Skills; Ear-Eye-Hand Phonics Kit; Happy Listening Time; Sound-Sight-Skills Kit

Educational Development Laboratories, 284 Pulaski Road, Huntington, NY 11744
Listen-Look-Learn Reading Program; Aud-X Program

Educational Progress Corporation; Bob Mank, Representative; PO Box 2691, Laguna Hills, CA 92653, (714) 545-3971
Audio Reading Progress Laboratory; EPC Reading Progress Lab

Follett Education Corporation; Don Oliver, Representative; 18216 Bayberry Way, Irvine, CA 92664, (714) 552-9074
Silly Listening Book; Sound/Order/Sense

Houghton Mifflin Company, 1 Beacon Street, Boston, MA 02107
Listen and Do; Listening and Learning

Instructional Materials and Equipment Distributors; Don Parson, Representative; 1520 Cotner, Los Angeles, CA 90025
Perceptual Communication Skills; Developing Auditory Awareness and Insight

Peter Pan Industries, West Coast Office, 15714 Garfield Avenue, Paramount, CA 90723
Read-along books with records; over one hundred literature titles

Rheem Califone Company, 5922 Bowcroft Street, PO Box 78567, Los Angeles, CA 90016
Califone Audio Reader; Califone Remedial Reading Program

Scholastic Book Services; Trudy Yeo, Representative; 6342 Newbury Drive, Huntington Beach, CA 92647, (714) 842-4614
Paperback titles K-12; records with some titles; tapes with some titles; Scholastic Listening Skills Program, 1-6

Science Research Associates, 3820 Fernwood Avenue, Orange, CA 92669, (714) 538-4021
Alphabet Learning; Listening-Doing-Learning; Phonics Express; Reading Lab: Listening Skill Builder; Tutor-tapes

Scott Foresman Company, 855 California Avenue, Palo Alto, CA 94304
Sounds Around Us; Talking Alphabet

Society for Visual Education, 1345 Diversey Parkway, Chicago, IL 60614
Learning Modules

Spoken Arts, Inc., 310 North Avenue, New Rochelle, NY 10801

Tapes Unlimited, 13001 Puritan Avenue, Detroit, MI 98227
Tapes Unlimited

Teaching Resources; Jim Whitney, Representative; 1125 Marchmont Street, Hacienda Heights, CA 91745, (213) 968-2554
Auditory Discriminations in Depth

Weston Woods Studios, Weston, CT 06880
Books, tapes, and recordings of the best in children's literature, including the Caldecott Award Winners

Appendix B
Classroom Listening
Materials

The following classroom listening materials are intended as a supplement to those presented in the text. They were collected and prepared by Julie M. T. Chan, California State University at Long Beach.

Suggestions for Assembling
Listening Center Kits

A. Contents
1. Six to eight copies of a single book title
2. One tape or record of story
3. Three folders:
   a) Worksheets (store ditto master here; run off as needed)
   b) Answer key
   c) Completed work
4. One manila envelope (10" X 13") for storage of above materials
   a) Label *flap* side
   b) Color code with signal dots for easy identification
      (1) Warm colors: Red, reading instructional tapes (skills development or practice); Orange, language arts; Yellow, literature tapes
      (2) Cool colors: Blue, music (enrichment); Green, science, math; Purple, social studies
B. Storage
1. Store materials in soft-drink cartons cut sideways or in a metal or wooden file
C. Instructional Tape Format
1. Introduction
2. Practice item and check (to be sure the student is on the right track)
3. Body of tape
4. Self-check (answers on tape for immediate knowledge of results—reinforcement)
5. Departing directions (very important—or the children may disturb the rest of the class as they leave the listening center). Example of directions:

Before you take off your headset, please check to see if you wrote your name on your paper. Next, put your crayon back in the crayon can. Now, think of *two* things that you can do when

135

you return to your desk. Remember, it should be something quiet so you won't disturb the other boys and girls while they are working.

A Sample Instructional Tape:
Sounds around Us

Objective. Given a common sound from the everyday environment, the child should be able to recognize it, identify the object from which it came, and indicate the answer on the worksheet provided (see Figure 19).

Introduction. "Today, we are going to see how well you listen. You will hear sounds that are all around you every day. Your job will be to see if you recognize these sounds."

Practice item. "For practice, let's do the first sound together. Look closely at your worksheet. Look at each picture. Here is sound number one. Are you able to find the picture of the object that makes this sound? When you have found the right picture, write the number—one—in the little box next to the object that makes this sound. Let's check to see if you are on the right track. Did you write number one in the box next to the picture of the *bell*? It is the last picture in row one. If you did, you are correct."

Body of the tape. "Now let's do the rest of the sounds. We will check our work when we have heard *all* of the sounds."

2. whistle	10. phonograph music
3. news on the radio	11. keys jingling
4. door opening and closing	12. pencil being sharpened
5. alarm clock ticking; ringing	13. stapler going through sheets of paper
6. water dripping from faucet	
7. hammering	14. clapping
8. typing	15. phone ringing
9. telephone dial tone	16. sawing

Check your work (immediate reinforcement). "Let's see how well you listened. Put your pencil down and take a crayon to check your work. Write a *C* next to the correct answer and an *X* if your answer is incorrect."

Sound No. 1 was a _____. Write a *C* if you were right, an *X* if you were not.

Sound No. 2 was a _____. Write a *C* if you were right, an *X* if you were not.

Departure directions. "Before you take off your headset, please check to see if you wrote your name on your paper. Next, put your crayon back in the crayon can. Now, I want you to think of *two* things that you can do when you return to your desk. Remember, it should be something quiet so you won't disturb the other boys and girls while they are working. As you leave the listening center, you may place your worksheet in the folder that says 'Completed Work.' Shhhhh! Now very quietly take off your headsets, lay them on the table where you are sitting, and tiptoe very quietly back to your desk. Over and out."

Fig. 19. A student worksheet for use with the Sounds around Us lesson.

A Sample Instructional Tape:
Listening to Follow the Dots

Purpose. Auditory memory; sequencing; directionality (left-right, top-bottom).

Behavioral objective. Given four points or dots, the student is able to listen to directions and follow them to make a diagram, object, or design, using the dots.

Materials. Pencils, dittoed worksheets (see Figure 20), tape, tape recorder, listening post.

Introduction. "How well are you able to follow directions? Well, let's begin by writing your name and today's date at the top of your paper. [Teacher: silently count to ten while tape is running.] Fine.

"Today, we'll see how well you are able to follow directions by making pictures or objects from the four dots that are in each of the squares on your sheet of paper. You will need to listen carefully so you'll know what lines to draw and in what order."

Practice item. "First, let's find box number one. Found it? Yes, it's the box with the number one and a square around that number. Now look at each of the four dots. Do you see the dot with the letter *T* next to it? That's the top dot. Now find the bottom dot. Yes, it's the one with a *B* under it. Next find the dot on the left; it has an *L* next to it, which stands for *left*. The last dot has an *R*, which means it is the dot on the right.

"OK. Let's draw something that most of you can play with. Start at the dot at the top by placing your pencil there. Now draw a line straight down to the dot at the bottom. Next, find the dot on the left and put your pencil there. Draw a line from this dot straight across to the dot on the right. Go back up to the dot at the top. Draw a line from this dot at the top to the dot on the left. Now continue from this dot on the left to the bottom dot. Let's go back up to the dot at the top again. Place your pencil at this top dot and draw a line to the dot on the right; continue from this dot on the right to the bottom dot.

"Can you tell what you have drawn? Yes! It's a kite!" (Teacher: please silently count to five after each new direction; this gives the listener time to think and draw.)"

Body of tape. "Let's try another one! Please go to square number two. Place your pencil on the top dot. All set? Draw a line from the top dot all the way down to the bottom dot. Pick up your pencil and find the left dot. Put your pencil on the left dot and draw a line all the way across to the right dot. Stop. Go back to the left dot. Draw a line from this left dot to the top dot. Go back again to the left dot and draw a line to the bottom dot. What does this look like to you? A bow and arrow, perhaps?

"Let's try square number three now. Place your pencil on the top dot and draw a line over to the dot on the left. Go back up to the top dot. This time, draw a line to the right dot. Stop. Pick up your pencil and place it on the left dot. Draw a line from this left dot straight across to the dot on the right.

Form One
Four Dots (T–B, L–R)

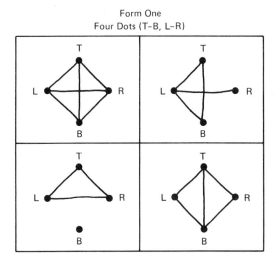

Fig. 20. A student worksheet for use with the Listening to Follow the Dots lesson.

What does this look like? Use your imagination! How does a three-cornered hat strike you?

"Now, let's do box number four. Let's begin by placing your pencil on the top dot. Draw a line straight down to the bottom dot. Pick up your pencil and place it on the top dot again. Draw a diagonal line (or slanted line) from the top dot to the left dot. Continue from this left dot to the bottom dot. Stop. Place your pencil on the top dot again. Make a diagonal line from the top dot to the dot on the right; continue from the dot on the right down to the bottom dot. Could this be the sandwich that you'll have for lunch?"

Departure directions. "Wouldn't it be fun to color these pictures that you have just drawn and add more details? You may do this when you go back to your desk. Now, quietly take off your earphones, lay them on the table where you are sitting, and *tiptoe* very quietly back to your desk. Over and out!"

A Sample Instructional Tape:
Word Identification

Objective. Students are given fifteen pairs of words; they should be able to recognize the vowel digraphs and indicate them by circling the answer on the worksheet.

Materials. For the teacher: (1) tape, (2) recorder and microphone, and (3) Ginn *Roads to Everywhere.* For the student: (1) pencils, (2) worksheets, (3) correction crayon, and (4) headsets.

Introduction. "Today, we are going to review vowel digraph sounds. Remember that digraphs are two vowels together that make one sound."

Practice item. "For practice, I shall say two words that contain the same vowel sound. You are to find the letter *group* that makes that sound and draw a circle around it.

"Look now at number one. My words are *play* and *day*. Listen to the vowel that can make that sound and draw a circle around it. [Pause five seconds.] You should have circled *ay*."

Body of lesson. "Now, proceed in the same way using the following pairs."

1. play	day	6. blew	new	11. now	growl
2. wait	tail	7. boat	coat	12. suit	fruit
3. sound	about	8. good	book	13. field	shield
4. boy	toy	9. blow	grow	14. freight	neighbor
5. caught	taught	10. boil	coin	15. boot	root

Self-check. "Let's check your paper to see how well you have done. If you do not have the correct group of letters circled, place an *X* on the wrong answer and *circle* the correct answer. Put your pencil back into the pencil can and take a crayon from the crayon can to check your work. Are you ready?"

1. ay	4. oy	7. oa	10. oi	13. ie
2. ai	5. au	8. oo	11. ow	14. ei
3. ou	6. ew	9. ow	12. ui	15. oo

Departure directions. (Whisper this part of the script.) "Before you take off your headsets, please check to see if you wrote your name on your paper. Next, place your crayon back in the crayon can. Now, I want you to think of *two* things that you can do when you return to your desk. Remember, it should be something quiet so you won't disturb the other girls and boys while they are working. As you leave the listening center, you may place your worksheet in the folder that says 'Completed Work.' Shhhh! Very quietly take off your headsets, lay them on the table, and *tiptoe* very quietly back to your desks. Over and out!"

Techniques and Their Uses in the Listening Center

I. Instruction that is used annually
   A. Individual instruction
      1. For high-ability students
      2. For low-ability students
   B. Reteaching a skill
      1. For those who have been absent
      2. For those who need to relearn
   C. Testing
      1. Practice for tests (pretest)
      2. The test itself

Review Lesson on Vowel Digraphs and Dipthongs

Name _____   Date _____

1.	ay	ea	ew	oy
2.	ea	ou	oi	ai
3.	oi	aw	ew	ou
4.	ay	ou	oy	aw
5.	ey	ew	ow	au
6.	aw	ow	ew	ei
7.	ai	oi	oa	aw
8.	oo	ou	oi	ui
9.	ea	ow	aw	ew
10.	ea	oi	aw	ew
11.	ew	ow	aw	ey
12.	ui	ew	aw	ey
13.	ea	ie	ew	oi
14.	aw	ow	ei	oo
15.	oi	aw	ew	oo

Fig. 21. In the Word Identification lesson, students circle the vowel digraph or dipthong contained in pairs of words read by the teacher.

II. Building listening skills
    A. On a one-to-one basis
    B. On a group basis
    C. Step-by-step instructions
    D. A series of instructions
III. Enjoying cultural experiences
    A. Music
    B. Literature or stories
IV. Creative thinking
    A. Open-ended or unfinished stories
    B. Problem solving
        1. Math
        2. Science
        3. Social Studies
    C. Discovery method
        1. Math
        2. Science
V. Children's recordings
    A. Plays, choral reading, oral interpretation of stories
    B. Measuring reading growth (oral)

Some Ideas for Using a Listening Center in the Areas
We Are Currently Teaching

I. Art and music
    A. Interpreting music through art
    B. Listening to a story and drawing
        1. A character in the story
        2. A favorite part of the story
    C. Listening to a story; just before it ends, stop and ask the children to make their own ending
II. Language arts
    A. Creative writing
        1. Tell a short problem story about friends. Have the children develop their own solutions
        2. Record a story but leave it unfinished. Have the children create their own ending
    B. English
        1. How to use a dictionary
        2. How to make a book report
    C. Foreign language resources. Some school systems have complete tapes on conversational Spanish and French, as well as songs and dances of these cultures
    D. Listening to stories for enjoyment
    E. Radio plays
    F. Spelling
        1. Individualized spelling program
        2. Weekly tests for regular spelling programs

III. Math
   A. Mr. Arithmetic number fact drill
      1. Addition
      2. Subtraction
      3. Multiplication
      4. Division
      5. Percentage
   B. Guided seatwork
   C. Math games
   D. Story problems
   E. Discovery method using Cuisenaire Rods
IV. Reading
   A. Diagnostic tests
   B. Science Research Associates *Listening Skill Builders*
   C. Enrichment activity to follow a reading-group story
   D. Introduction of new words in reading
   E. Guided seatwork
   F. Phonics lessons (commercial records are available)
   G. Listening to a story to master sequence and retention skills
   H. Recording improvement in expression in oral reading. Children enjoy hearing their own voices. A measure of growth in this area for the pupil, parent, and teacher can be made by comparing reading samples from the beginning of the year with those from the end of the year
   I. Reading games
V. Science
   A. Individual science experiments
   B. How to record data
   C. Listening to read-aloud excerpts from science books and learning to draw conclusions
VI. Social studies
   A. How to make reports
   B. Practicing reporting
   C. Reading selections from books
   D. Interviewing a resource person who is unable to visit the class and recording the interview

Notes

Chapter One

1. *Masking* refers to the obscuring of one sound by another.

2. *Encoding* refers to the process of transforming a received message into signals or symbols, as when an individual transforms his or her intentions into signals in a communication system, usually by an oral or written symbol system, but also by gestures. Encoding may include *recoding* or transformation into several encodings, as when an individual writes out a telegram that is then transformed by another person into electric signals. These signals might then be transformed into another language and sent. The message might also be recoded into another related oral dialect as it passes on. Decoding refers to the process by which receiving individuals transform stimulating signals into meaningful messages.

3. The term *auditory discrimination* usually refers to the ability to notice separate, minute sounds in spoken words. For example, a third-grade child reads the word *must* as *mus.* The teacher says, "You mean *must,* don't you," and the child replies, "Sure, *mus.* That's what I said." Poor discrimination, poor pronunciation, and poor reading tend to go together (Harris, 1969). There appears to be little relationship, however, between auditory discrimination and the scores on most intelligence tests (e.g., Witkin, 1969).

4. Visual graphs of frequencies that make up vowel sounds suggest that a child needs fine discriminations in order to separate sounds that distinguish one word from another, such as *bat* from *pat.*

5. Also see Sanders (1977), *Auditory Perception of Speech: An Introduction to Principles and Problems,* Chapter 10, "Speech Perception and Reading." See Neville and Pugh (1974) for a comparison of children's errors during reading and during listening to the same cloze tests (discussed in chapter four of this book).

6. Also see Smith (1977), Lundsteen (1977), Lundsteen and Berstein-Tarrow (in press), Goodman and Goodman (1977), and Jackson, Robinson, Halbert, and Dale (1976), Waller (1977), Stammer (1977).

7. For activities, see the Russell and Russell reference and Schlawin, Chew, and Crabtree (1975), Halley (1975), and Lundsteen (1976b).

8. An example of early research on this question is Carver (1935). Also see Delile in Duker (1968).

9. Inner speech also occurs during speaking and reading. Auditory word impressions traveling at high speeds are largely received unconsciously (Brown, 1954).

10. Another commonly used word for *receiving* (with comprehension) is *decoding* (for example, while reading and listening). Another word commonly used synonymously with the term *expressing* (or sending) is *encoding* (e.g., while speaking or writing).

Chapter Two

1. The term *auding,* developed by D. P. Brown and students (1954), appears, for example, in the *Dictionary of Psychological and Psychoanalytical Terms.* Some writers in the field refer to the term from time to time, though it has not attained widespread use. For that reason, the term will not be used in this book, especially since, in the context of the language arts, speech symbols is usually the intended meaning.

2. For reviews and research on speeded-up (compressed) speech, see Duker (1968, 1969), Foulke (1968), Friedman and Johnson (1968), Sticht (1969, 1971), Thomas and Rossiter (1972), Short (1973), and Silverstone (1974). See also the section on attention further on in this book. For more on masking and competing messages, see, for example, Broadbent in Duker (1968).

3. *Kinesics* is the term used to refer to these movements. For an example, see the work of Key (1975, 1977).

4. See the sections on listening materials in chapter five. One variation in the listening diet is to have children listen to imaginative sounds on a record, such as *Sounds and Images* by Bert Cunningham and E. Paul Torrance (Ginn and Co.).

5. The human range of conscious auditory reception is about 15,000 to 20,000 vibrations or cycles per second.

6. An audiometer is an instrument for testing acuity of hearing. Some types use a vacuum-tube oscillator regulated to produce a series of tones at various points throughout the audibility range, each at various intensity levels above normal. Measurements of hearing loss are shown in terms of decibels or of percentage of normal hearing sensitivity. For informal tests see Kough and deHaan (1955).

7. A common procedure in speeding up the rate of speech is to cut out small segments of sound; speech rate is decreased by adding small segments. The center for rate-controlled recording at the University of Kentucky does much of this work. See Thomas and Rossiter (1972), Short (1973), and Silverstone (1975).

8. Slurvien was devised by William Tiffany, of the University of Washington, for his Phonetic Listening Test (1963).

9. The alphabet of the International Phonetic Association is found, for example, in the front of such dictionaries as *Webster's New Collegiate,* together with information on symbolization of stress and length of duration

in pronunciation. This alphabet is designed to include the most important sounds occurring in the languages of the world.

10. Comprehension is developed further in chapter three of this book.

11. Actually, passive listening does not belong in this tenth step, which is described as highly conscious.

12. There are high correlations among scores on measures of attention, focusing, tracking, discrimination, sorting, scanning, and sequencing, perhaps because of the almost simultaneous occurrence of these processes (Witkin, 1969).

Chapter Three

1. Much of the next section is influenced by Kellogg's work elaborated in the chapter titled "Listening" in the first edition of *Guiding Children's Language Learning,* edited by Pose Lamb (Dubuque, Iowa: William C. Brown, 1971).

2. This includes recognition, figure-ground perception, sequencing, synthesis, and analysis.

3. One prospective teacher commented on this matrix classification of listening skills, saying that it specifically provides a framework for ordering the small number of "known" listening skills, and then, "in one fell swoop," it was possible to determine the rest of them. She liked that.

4. Much of the taxonomy of the affective domain (Krathwohl and others, 1964) could be related to listening skills pertinent to attitudes, values, feeling tone, emotion, and acceptance or rejection.

5. This idea for a learning center is adapted from a presentation by Cheryl Biles, Extended Teaching Staff, San Joaquin School District, East Irvine, California. See the listening and creative problem-solving activities at the end of chapter three. See also Choate (1974).

6. The skills that demand a high degree of awareness during listening should not foster "predatory" listening, e.g., the kind that takes place during some congressional committee hearings.

7. Other two-way classifications of listening skills are: (a) accuracy of reception and mental reaction and reflection; (b) cognitive and affective; (c) knowledge of specifics (first division of Bloom taxonomy) and levels higher than knowledge of specifics (the rest of the Bloom taxonomy).

8. This section is based on a discussion in Bormuth (1970a and b, 1975).

9. Some tasks might deviate so much from general practice that finding analogous practice opportunities would be extremely difficult. This would make the value of the task questionable. The learning of certain grammatical rules, where the same examples have been passed on for generations, is an extreme example.

10. Diagrams of hierarchies usually are read from bottom to top, but, in order to make a quick association with the elaborated objective, the order here is from the top down.

11. This analysis is based on work by Flavel (1968). Also see the important study by Keyes and others (1975).

12. Flavel (1968) and Keyes (1975) have found evidence of development in role-taking.

13. Sarbin (1954).

14. Adapted from Flavel (1968).

15. Flavel (1968).

16. Adapted from Brown (1954) and Carroll (1968).

17. Caution: these examples are admittedly artificial and represent diagnostic tasks. A superior and more developmentally oriented approach is to be ready to note and reinforce the same parts of the problem-solving process when they occur spontaneously during the free play or other self-directed activity of the child. It is preferable to capitalize on actual problems as they occur; then the teacher's questions can help the child to see the significant features of the problem-solving process.

18. See the problem-solving lessons in *Ideas Into Practice* (Lundsteen, 1976b). This section on listening to solve problems is inspired in part by the research of John F. Feldhusen and others at Purdue University.

19. See the listening lessons in *Ideas Into Practice* (Lundsteen, 1976b) for examples of roadblocks (distortions), helpful concepts, and activities.

Chapter Five

1. Also see the reference to criteria by Tyler, Klein, and Michael (1971) and the review of materials by Deugau (1969).

2. Most items on materials and techniques that appeared in Lundsteen (1969c) have not been repeated here. The *Listening Bibliography* by Duker (1968) included 32 entries on materials, 143 on techniques, and 300 annotated entries on the teaching of listening.

3. For information write to Roger J. Schulte, Assistant Superintendent, Alameda County School Department, 224 W. Winton Ave., Hayward, California 94544.

4. PO Box 564, Lenox Hill Station, New York, New York 10021. Also see Siebert (1972).

5. The author wishes to express appreciation to Charles F. Kenney, District Superintendent, Santa Ana, California, Unified and Junior College Districts, for reacting to this section.

References

Abrams, A. G. "The Relation of Listening and Reading Comprehension to Skill in Message Structuralization." *Journal of Communication* 16 (1968): 116-25.

A study designed to test the hypothesis that the ability to structuralize, to recognize the structure of a written message, correlates significantly and positively with listening and with reading comprehension.

Adams, F. J. "Evaluation of a Listening Program Designed to Develop Awareness of Propaganda Techniques." Ph.D. dissertation, Boston University, 1968.

Evaluates a series of recorded lessons designed to make tenth-grade pupils aware of propaganda techniques.

Ammon, P. R. *Aspects of Speech Comprehension by Children and Adults: Two Experimental Studies of the Comprehension of Sentences.* USOE Final Report, Project No. 7-I-114, 1969. [ED 037 643]

Results imply that subjects' (fifth grade and college) expectations as to the probable content influenced the manner in which they interpreted sentences that varied systematically in syntactic structure and content. Results suggest that even after a brief delay the listener must reconstruct the exact wording of a sentence from a deeper interpretation. Variations in age and sex indicate the need for considering individual differences in the listening comprehension process.

Anastasiow, N., and I. B. Espinosa. "Development of a Spanish Listening Comprehension Test and Evaluation of the Elementary Spanish Television Instruction." *California Journal of Education Research* 17 (1966): 12-21.

Anderson, R. C. "Control of Student Mediating Processes during Verbal Learning and Instruction." *Review of Educational Research* 40 (June 1970): 349-69.

Ball, S., and G. A. Bogatz. *The Modern American Electric-Pragmatic Design: "Sesame Street" and the "Electric Company."* Princeton, N.J.: Educational Testing Service, n.d.

Discusses the problems of testing this kind of listening experience.

Bassett, R. "Minimal Speaking and Listening Competencies for High School Graduates: Status of Research." Paper presented at the Annual Meeting of the American Educational Research Association, Toronto, Canada, April 1978.

Bednarz, B. "Project Sound Makes It." *Elementary English* 48 (January 1971): 86-89.
   Suggests how listening to sound is related to creative writing and gives a list of thirty-one musical selections as starters.

Bernthal, E. S. "The Listening-Viewing Center as a Means of Motivating Original Work in Writing and Speaking English." In *Classroom Practices in Teaching English, 1967-68,* edited by A. J. Beeler and D. W. Emery, pp. 3-5. Champaign, Ill.: NCTE, 1967.
   Children need language arts activities that are meaningful and purposeful. One way to do this is to program them into the Listening-Viewing Center so that materials can be shared with other children.

Blackburn, S. F. "The Construction, the Implementation, and the Evaluation of a Title I Primary Grade Listening Program." Ph.D. dissertation, University of Mississippi, 1976.
   An experimental group (N = 110) improved significantly over control group on Cooperative Primary Tests on listening and on author's Listening Rating Scale.

Bloom, A. K. "Taught, Not Caught." *English Journal* 43 (October 1954): 367-70.
   Gives detailed unit in which students learn criteria for evaluation of TV and radio news broadcasts.

Bloom, B. S., ed. *Taxonomy of Educational Objectives, the Classification of Educational Goals, Handbook I: Cognitive Domain.* New York: David McKay, 1956.

Bordie, J. G. "Language Tests and Linguistically Different Learners: The Sad State of the Art." *Elementary English* 47 (October 1970): 814-28. Also in T. D. Horn, ed., *Research Bases for Oral Language Instruction.* Urbana, Ill.: NCTE for National Conference on Research in English, 1971.
   Examines the measuring techniques for identifying the characteristics of linguistically different learners (e.g., attention span, mental ability).

Bormuth, J. R. "An Operational Definition of Comprehension Instruction." In *Psycholinguistics and the Teaching of Reading,* edited by K. S. Goodman and J. T. Fleming. Newark, Del.: International Reading Association, 1969. For a treatment in depth see J. R. Bormuth, *On a Theory of Achievement Test Items.* Chicago: University of Chicago Press, 1970.

Bormuth, J. R. "The Cloze Procedure: Literacy in the Classroom." In *Help for the Reading Teacher: New Directions in Research,* edited by W. D. Page. Urbana, Ill.: National Conference on Research in English and ERIC/RCS, 1975.

Bormuth, J. R., J. Carr, J. Manning, and D. Pearson. "Children's Comprehension of Between-and-Within-Sentence Syntactic Structures." *Journal of Educational Psychology* 33 (1970): 349-57. [ED 028 902]
   A study investigating comprehension skills of fourth-grade children of average achievement. Comprehension was found to be low on appar-

ently simple and basic comprehension skills. Implications might be drawn for listening.

Brewer, J. M. "Hidden Language: Ghetto Children Know What They Are Talking About." *New York Times Magazine,* 25 December 1966, pp. 32-35.

Broadbent, D. E. "Attention and the Perception of Speech." *Scientific American,* April 1962, pp. 143-51.

Broadbent, D. E. "The Well Ordered Mind." *American Educational Research Journal* 33 (November 1966): 281-95.

Brown, D. P. "Auding as the Primary Language Ability." Ph.D. dissertation, Stanford University, 1954.
    Now a classic theoretical study by the man who coined the word *auding.* Contains activities and evaluative techniques for the high school level. The references made to studies of aphasia are taken from this source.

Brown, J. I. "The Construction of a Diagnostic Test of Listening Comprehension." *Journal of Experimental Education* 18 (December 1949): 139-46.
    Describes procedures related to the construction of the Brown-Carlsen Listening Comprehension Test.

Brown, R. A. *The Tyranny of Noise.* New York: St. Martin's Press, 1970.
    Presents what noise is and what it does to you. The author is director of Citizens for a Quieter City, Inc., in New York, and a crusader against noise.

Bruner, J. S. "Personality Dynamics and the Process of Perceiving." In *Perception: An Approach to Personality,* edited by R. Blake and G. Ramsay. New York: Ronald Press, 1951.

Bursuk, L. Z. "Sensory Mode of Lesson Presentation as a Factor in the Reading Comprehension Improvement of Adolescent Retarded Readers." Paper presented to the American Educational Research Association, New York, February 1971.
    Recommends screening to see if retarded students prefer the aural or visual mode of presentation. If the teacher cannot obtain this information, then he or she should integrate both modes in teaching.

Caccavo, E. "The Listening Comprehension Level of an Informal Reading Inventory as a Predictor of Intelligence of Elementary School Children." Ph.D. dissertation, New York University, 1968. [ED 040 997]

Caffrey, J. C. "Auding Ability as a Function of Certain Psychometric Variables." Ph.D. dissertation, University of California, Berkeley, 1953.
    Gives a model of careful test construction in a now classic study at the high school level. The second definition in chapter two draws heavily on the pioneer work of this researcher.

Carroll, J. B. "A Factor Analysis of Two Foreign Language Aptitude Batteries." *Journal of General Psychology* 59 (1958): 3-19.

Carroll, J. B. "Development of Native Language Skills beyond the Early Years." Mimeographed. Princeton, N.J.: Educational Testing Service, June 1968.

Reviews the development of language competence and performance skills beyond the years of primary language acquisition, i.e., from about first grade on. One part focuses upon dimensions of individual differences that might be found in listening and shows that development is by no means complete upon school entry, although the normal child has substantial competence in the rules of his or her native language. Points out gaps in knowledge. Included in the book, *The Learning of Language,* edited by Carroll Reed, published by Appleton-Century-Crofts.

Carver, M. E. "Listening versus Reading." In *The Psychology of Radio,* edited by H. Cantril and G. W. Allport, pp. 159-80. New York: Harper, 1935.

Cazden, C. B. "Subcultural Differences in Child Language: An Interdisciplinary Review." *Merrill-Palmer Quarterly of Behavior and Development* 12 (1966): 185-219. [ED 011 325]

Chang, Y. C. C. "The Ability of Sixth Grade Pupils to Use Certain Verbal Context Clues in Listening and Reading." Ph.D. dissertation, University of Minnesota, 1968. [ED 040 998]

Choate, R. "Television's Children: Television Fare, Alias TV Dinners." *Learning: The Magazine for Creative Teaching,* vol. 2, no. 5 (1974): 39.

This feature on television appears in each issue. Check others.

Chomsky, C. S. "Stages in Language Development and Reading Exposure." *Harvard Educational Review* 42 (1972): 1-33.

Research supports the possible lifting effect of a challenging listening diet. High complexity of material read aloud to children was found to be closely associated with skill in comprehending complex sentence structure spoken to children five to ten years of age.

Conrad, R. "The Chronology of the Development of Covert Speech in Children." *Developmental Psychology* 5 (1971): 398-405.

Conrad, R. "Speech and Reading." In *Language by Ear and by Eye: The Relationships between Speech and Reading,* edited by J. F. Kavanaugh and I. G. Mattingly. Cambridge, Mass.: MIT Press, 1972.

Cooper, R. L. "The Ability of Deaf and Hearing Children to Apply Morphological Rules." Ph.D. dissertation, Columbia University, 1965.

Presents evidence based on test adapted from Berko of the importance of accessibility of spoken language in language development ages seven to nineteen. In applying derivational suffixes, for example, the average scores of nineteen-year-old deaf children were below the average scores of ten year olds who could hear.

Cottrill, T., and R. T. Alciatore. "A Comparison of Two Methods of Teaching Listening Comprehension to College Freshmen." *Western Speech,* vol. 33, no. 2 (1974): 117-123.

Cullinan, B. E., and C. W. Carmichael, eds. *Literature and Young Children.* Urbana, Ill.: NCTE, 1977.

Denson, T. A. "An Experimental Study of the Effect of a Listening Skills Training Program in Kindergarten on the Development of Pre-reading Skills." Ph.D. dissertation, University of Southern California, 1973.
    The results of two kinds of treatment—a structured listening skills program and story tapes—were found to be the same.

Desousa, A. N., and M. Cowles. "An Experimental Study to Determine the Efficacy of Specific Training in Listening." Paper presented at the Annual Meeting of the American Educational Research Association, Toronto, Canada, April 1978.

Deugau, D. "A Critical Bibliography of Listening Materials." *Alberta English* 9 (Fall 1969): 14-23.
    Evaluates eight phonograph records and tape recordings useful for listening instruction; specifies source, grade level, and cost and gives content summary.

Devine, T. G. "Listening." *Review of Educational Research* 37 (April 1967): 153-58.
    Reviews research on teaching of listening, factors affecting reading and listening, other correlational studies, and measures of listening.

Devine, T. G. "Reading and Listening: New Research Findings." *Elementary English* 45 (March 1968): 346-48.
    Reexamines the belief that instruction in listening (or reading) affects pupil competence in reading (or listening).

Devine, T. G. "Listening: What Do We Know after Fifty Years of Research and Theorizing?" *Journal of Reading,* vol. 21, no. 4 (1978): 269-304.

Devito, L. "Communications Program in Developing Basic Skills." Ph.D. dissertation, Boston University, 1977.

DiBiasio, M. "The Relationship of Listening and Reading in Grades 2, 4, and 6." Ph.D. dissertation, Boston University, 1977.

Di Vesta, F., and S. G. Gray. "Listening and Note Taking." *Journal of Educational Psychology,* vol. 63, no. 1 (1972): 6-14.

Doyle, A.-B. "Listening to Distraction: A Developmental Study of Selective Attention." *Journal of Experimental Child Psychology,* vol. 15, no. 1 (1973): 100-105.

Duker, S. *Listening: Readings.* Metuchen, N.J.: Scarecrow Press, 1966. (New volume, *Listening: Readings II,* 1971.)

Duker, S. *Listening Bibliography.* 2d ed. Metuchen, N.J.: Scarecrow Press, 1968.
    Represents an updating of the 1964 annotated bibliography; 1,332 references are listed. An invaluable service.

Duker, S. "Listening." In *Encyclopedia of Educational Research,* 4th ed., edited by R. L. Ebel, pp. 747-52. New York: Macmillan, 1969. [ED 029 896]

> Reviews the extent of listening, scope of the literature, relationships to listening, teaching of listening, measurement of listening, and listening to compressed or speeded speech.

Duker, S. "Teaching Listening: Recently Developed Programs and Materials." *Training and Development Journal,* May 1970, pp. 11-14.

> Surveys available resources at the adult level.

Durrell, D. D., and H. A. Murphy. "The Auditory Discrimination Factor in Reading Readiness and Reading Disability." *Education* 73 (1953): 556-60.

> Durrell and Murphy suggest that intensive instruction in auditory perception removes most, if not all, of the advantage that girls appear to have over boys in first grade reading success. Results from Kellogg's (1966) study suggest the same. Auditory discrimination and ability to listen to discourse contribute to reading success.

Ebel, R. L. "The Paradox of Educational Testing." *Measurement in Education,* vol. 7, no. 4 (1976): 1-7.

Edfeldt, A. W. *Silent Speech and Silent Reading.* Chicago: University of Chicago Press, 1960.

Edgar, K. F. "The Validation of Four Methods of Improving Listening Ability." Ph.D. dissertation, University of Pittsburgh, 1961.

Educational Testing Service. "Listening Levels 1, 2, 3, 4." In *Sequential Tests of Educational Progress* (1957). "Listening." In *Cooperative Primary Tests* (1967). Princeton, N. J.: Educational Testing Service, Cooperative Test Division.

> Consists of two alternate forms for primary grades through college. Assumed subabilities: plain-sense comprehension, interpretation, evaluation, and application. Graded tests increase in vocabulary difficulty, grammatical complexity, complexity of subject matter, and reasoning abilities.

Erway, E. A. "The Development of Programed Materials for Teaching Cognitive Listening Skills in a Speech Laboratory in the Beginning Speech Course at Hunter College." Ph.D. dissertation, Columbia University, 1966. In "Abstracts of Dissertations in the Field of Speech," edited by M. Nelson. *Speech Monographs* 34 (August 1967): 316.

> The purpose of the project was to develop programed materials in listening to public speaking for a beginning course. The behavioral goal of the linear program was the identification within contemporary speech samples of the central idea of the speech, the main divisions, the pattern of organization, the supporting material, motive appeals, and characteristics of language.

Farrell, M., and S. H. Flint. "Are They Listening?" *Childhood Education* 43 (May 1967): 528-29.
> Suggests the need for listening with a purpose. Every activity which includes environmental sound provides an opportunity for listening-learning experiences. Several musical games are described to teach discrimination between pitches, timbre, and quality of tone; to recognize tempo or speech changes; and to identify likeness or difference in rhythm and duration.

Flavel, J. H., and others. *The Development of Role-Taking and Communication Skills in Children.* New York: Wiley, 1968. [ED 027 082]
> Deals with the application of conceptual abilities to social-interpersonal as opposed to nonsocial, physical tasks. Shows how the child makes use of information about the receiver in devising and transmitting effective messages to others. Not only investigates a dimension neglected by Piaget, but also seeks to find ways to assist development.

Francis, P. S. "A Comparison of the Effectiveness of Three Oral Language Systems in Improving the Receptive Language of Kindergarten Children." Ph.D. dissertation, North Texas State University, 1978.

Frase, L. T. "Boundary Conditions for Mathemagenic Behaviors." *Review of Educational Research* 40 (June 1970): 337-47.
> Reviews research on orienting directions, e.g., use of questions, which get the reader to respond to certain aspects of a text. Examines position in text, closeness of the question to text, and type of question. Suggestions for needed study are relevant to spoken material.

French, J. W. "The Description of Aptitude and Achievement Tests in Terms of Rotated Factors." *Psychometric Monograph No. 5.* Chicago: University of Chicago Press, 1951.

Friedman, H. L., and R. L. Johnson. "Compressed Speech Correlates of Listening Ability." *Journal of Communication* 18 (September 1968): 207-18.
> Whole issue devoted to compressed speech. Includes bibliography of dissertations and master's theses.

Gall, M. D. "The Use of Questions in Teaching." *Review of Educational Research* 40 (December 1970): 707-21.
> A comprehensive review of classifications regarding type of question, teacher practices, student behavior, and programs designed to change teacher questioning behavior. Implications for the listening program may be drawn. One section deplores the fact that there is little research on pupil questions, possibly because pupils are not encouraged to ask them.

Gantt, W. N., R. M. Wilson, and C. M. Dayton. "An Initial Investigation of the Relationship between Syntactical Divergency and the Listening Comprehension of Black Children." *Reading Research Quarterly,* vol. 10, no. 2 (1974-75): 74-75.
> A caution on the preparation of dialect materials.

Gephart, W. J. *Application of the Convergence Technique to Basic Studies of the Reading Process.* USOE Final Report, Project No. 8-0737. Bloomington, Ind.: Phi Delta Kappa, 1970. [ED 037 587]

Appendix B is devoted to a definition of the reading process. The second chapter of this book draws heavily on the techniques used in Gephart's appendix and is intended to complement earlier work on reading. The appendix also includes a flow chart of Kenneth Goodman's model of reading, an inspiration for the model of listening presented in this book.

Glasser, T. L. "On Readability and Listenability." *ETC.: A Review of General Semantics,* vol. 32, no. 2 (1975): 138-42.

Warns that too much concern for brevity (e.g., short words), as measured by the Flesch readability formula and the Fang listenability formula, may unnecessarily restrict the use of symbols, may promote clarity at the expense of precision, and may be highly "listenable" with little information value.

Goldstein, H. "Reading and Listening Comprehension at Various Controlled Rates." *Contributions to Education,* No. 821. New York: Bureau of Publications, Teachers College, Columbia University, 1940.

An early, classic, and elegantly done study comparing reading and listening as a function of rate of presentation. Used 7 rates of presentation, the highest of which was 322 words per minute. One of the first studies to suggest that people can listen at a faster rate and not lose much in the way of comprehension.

Goodman, K. S., and O. S. Niles. *Reading: Process and Program.* Champaign, Ill.: NCTE, 1970. [ED 045 664]

Goodman presents a framework of comprehension, the only genuine objective of reading. The present model of listening behavior draws heavily on the original flow chart constructed at a USOE meeting referred to in the Gephart reference.

Goodman, K. S., and Y. M. Goodman. "Learning about Psycholinguistic Processes by Analyzing Oral Reading." *Harvard Educational Review* 77 (1977): 317-333.

Goolsby, T. M., and R. A. Lasco. "Training Non-Readers in 'Listening Achievement.'" *Journal of Learning Disabilities* 3 (1970): 44-47.

Five-year-old children (average population) were given differing kinds of training in listening using four stories, one per day. Treatment 1 pupils were questioned after each story and told whether or not their answers were right or wrong (immediate feedback). Treatment 2 pupils received questions but no knowledge of their results. Treatment 3 pupils were not even questioned. In an earlier study no feedback to deprived Head Start children resulted in significantly lower listening achievement. The implication for the children in the earlier study was that ability to answer questions on material improved when knowledge of results or feedback was given. This feedback may serve the function of advanced organizer for the next task in the case of less verbal children. No significant differences were found for the short training sessions for average children.

Gotkin, L. G., and F. Fendiller. "Listening Centers in the Kindergarten." *Audiovisual Instruction* 10 (January 1965): 24-26.
Advocates a classroom listening center with tape recorders to enable disadvantaged children to hear "school language" as distinguished from their own. Stresses minimal distraction in the center.

Gratz, E. W. "Goal: Maxi-Listening." *English Journal* 62 (1973): 268-71.

Graves, D. R. "Children's Writing: Research Directions and Hypotheses Based upon an Examination of the Writing Processes of Seven-Year-Old Children." Ph.D. dissertation, State University of New York at Buffalo, 1973. [ED 095 586]

Guilford, J. P. *The Nature of Human Intelligence.* New York: McGraw-Hill, 1967.
An elaborate concept of the nature of intelligence. Describes more than one hundred separate aspects of cognitive ability by a sort of "periodic table" of these factors. Each represents a particular combination of certain types of mental "operation," "content," and "product." Attempts to identify the process in the successful performance of mental tasks.

Gupta, W., and C. Stern. "Comparative Effectiveness of Speaking vs. Listening in Improving Spoken Language of Disadvantaged Young Children." *The Journal of Experimental Education* 38 (Fall 1969): 54-57. [ED 029 689]

Hall, W. S., and R. O. Freedle. "A Developmental Investigation of Standard and Nonstandard English Among Black and White Children." *Human Development* 16 (1973): 440-64.

Harris, T. L. "Reading." In *Encyclopedia of Educational Research,* edited by R. L. Ebel. New York: Macmillan, 1969.
See section on physiological aspects (p. 1083) for discussion of auditory acuity, discrimination, memory, silent speech, and reading.

Hayakawa, S. I. "Who Is Bringing Up Your Children?" *ETC.: A Review of General Semantics* 25 (September 1968): 299-308.
Discusses the impact of television upon children.

Heider, F. K., and G. M. Heider. "A Comparison of Sentence Structure of Deaf and Hearing Children." *Psychological Monographs* 52 (1940): 42-103.

Helm, S. M. "Impossible Mission." *Elementary English* 50 (1973): 546-48.
Clever use of theme from the television series "Mission Impossible"; students listen to tape-recorded "special assignments" to be carried out.

Hoetker, J. *Dramatics and the Teaching of Literature.* NCTE/ERIC Studies in the Teaching of English. Champaign, Ill.: National Council of Teachers of English, 1969. [ED 028 165]
Has a section on uses of drama in the elementary school.

Hogan, R., and N. Henley. "A Test of the Empathy-Effective Communication Hypothesis." Report No. 84. USOE Grant No. OEC 2-7-061610-0207. Baltimore, Md.: Johns Hopkins University, Center for Social Organization of Schools, 1970.

The assumption is that empathy or role taking is essential if effective information exchange is to occur between persons. The researchers used an objective measure of empathy and an encoding-decoding task with university students to simulate the communication process. A consistent and significant relationship was found between measures of encoding and empathy.

Horowitz, M. W. "Organizational Processes Underlying Differences between Listening and Reading as a Function of Complexity of Material." *Journal of Communication* 18 (1968): 37-46.

Suggests listening is freer from the stimulus than reading and more prone to distort the material conveyed, i.e., it is a looser and less inhibited process. It can also be more in tune with thought as it occurs than reading.

Houston, M. D. "A Language Arts Program for a Fourth Grade of Culturally Deprived Children." Master's thesis, East Tennessee State University, 1964.

Gives suggestions for the teacher on direction giving, questioning, give-and-take conversation, and the nonverbal ways of communicating of the children in this study.

Ironsmith, N., and G. J. Whitehurst. "How Children Learn to Listen: The Effects of Modeling Feedback Styles on Children's Performance in Referential Communication." *Developmental Psychology* 14 (1978): 546-54.

Jackson, N. E., H. B. Robinson, and P. S. Dale. *Cognitive Development in Young Children: A Report for Teachers.* Washington, D.C.: U.S. Department of Health, Education, and Welfare, National Institute of Education, 1976.

Johnson, K. R., and H. D. Simons. "Black Children and Reading." *Phi Delta Kappan,* 53 (January 1972): 288-90.

Johnson, R. L., and H. L. Friedman. "Optimal Strategies for Listening, II: Training of Component Skills." Paper presented at the Fifteenth Annual Convention, International Reading Association, 1970. In *Abstracts,* edited by J. S. Nemeth. Newark, Del.: IRA, 1970.

Presents effective listening skills through a formal systems analysis such that listening situations can be defined in terms of operations that produce preferred outcomes. Instructional units, prepared for ages ten to fourteen, were evaluated in a school in Philadelphia. After use of a specially developed battery of listening measures, significant pretest-post-test differences suggested effectiveness of the instruction.

Kavanaugh, J. F., and I. G. Mattingly, eds. *Language by Ear and by Eye: The Relationships between Speech and Reading.* Cambridge, Mass.: MIT Press, 1972.

Kellogg, R. E. "A Study of the Effect of a First Grade Listening Instructional Program upon Achievement in Listening and Reading." USOE Cooperative Research Project 6-8468. San Diego, Calif.: Department of Education, San Diego County, 1966. [ED 012 232]

Kelly, C. M. "Listening: Complex of Activities—and a Unitary Skill?" Reply by C. T. Brown, *Speech Monographs* 34 (November 1967): 455-66.
Cautions and directions for research. Raises questions about the state of knowledge basic to listening instruction.

Key, M. R. *Paralanguage and Kinesics: Nonverbal Communication.* Metuchen, N.J.: Scarecrow Press, 1975.

Key, M. R. *Nonverbal Communication: A Research Guide and Bibliography.* Metuchen, N.J.: Scarecrow Press, 1977.

Keyes, B. J., et al. "The Development of Listener Competence." Paper presented at the Biennial Meeting of the Society for Research in Child Development, Denver, Colorado, April 1975. [ED 115 359]

Kirkton, C. M. "NCTE/ERIC Report: Classroom Dramatics—Developing Oral Language Skills." *Elementary English* 48 (February 1971): 254-61.

Kirshner, G. " 'Start Where the Child Is'—Using Television to Teach the Child." *Elementary English* 46 (November 1969): 955-58.

Klee, L. E. "Larger Horizons for the Child: A Fourth Grade Experiment." *Social Education* 13 (February 1949): 69-71.
Demonstrates that stereotypes of foreigners remain difficult to change through social education.

Klinzing, D. G. "Listening Comprehension of Pre-School Age Children as a Function of Rate of Presentation, Sex, and Age." *Speech Teacher* 21 (March 1972): 86-92.

Kough, J., and R. deHaan. *Identifying Children with Special Needs: Teacher's Guidance Handbook, Elementary School Education.* Vol. 1. Chicago, Ill.: Science Research Associates, 1955.
Contains informal tests of hearing.

Krathwohl, D. R., B. S. Bloom, and B. B. Masia. *Taxonomy of Educational Objectives, the Classification of Educational Goals, Handbook II: Affective Domain.* New York: David McKay, 1964.

LaBerge, D. "Beyond Auditory Coding." In *Language by Ear and by Eye: The Relationships between Speech and Reading,* edited by J. F. Kavanaugh and I. G. Mattingly. Cambridge, Mass.: MIT Press, 1972.

Lane, P. K., and M. S. Miller. "Listening: Learning for Underachieving Adolescents." *Journal of Reading,* no. 7 (April 1972): 488-91.

Lasky, E. Z., B. Jay, and M. Hanz-Ehrman. "Meaningful and Linguistic Variables in Auditory Processing." *Journal of Learning Disabilities* 8 (1975): 570-77.

Lasser, M. "Sound Activities." *Media and Methods* 10 (December 1973): 20-21, 46.

Liberman, A. M., I. G. Mattingly, and M. T. Turvey. "Language Codes and Memory Codes." In *Coding Processes in Human Memory,* edited by A. W. Melton and E. Martin. Washington, D. C.: V. H. Winston, 1972.

Lundgren, R. E., and R. J. Shavelson. "Effects of Listening Training on Teacher Listening and Discussion Skills." *California Journal of Educational Research* 25 (September 1974): 205-18.
During an examination of secondary level teacher-training students at Stanford University, listening skills were defined as the teacher's ability to extract information completely and accurately. The trainees' ability to use key words in summarizing a discussion was the most reliable measure of listening. Improvement came with training.

Lundsteen, S. W. "A Model of the Teaching-Learning Process for Assisting Development of Children's Thinking during Communication." *Journal of Communication* 18 (1968): 412-35. (a)

Lundsteen, S. W. "Language Arts in the Elementary School." In *Teaching for Creative Endeavor,* edited by W. B. Michael. Bloomington: Indiana University Press, 1968. (b)
A creative problem-solving approach to teaching listening. Describes activities and gives some brief notes on what research says to the teacher.

Lundsteen, S. W. "Research in Critical Listening and Thinking: A Recommended Goal for Future Research." *Journal of Research and Development in Education* 3 (Fall 1969): 119-33. (a)

Lundsteen, S. W. "Critical Listening Research and Development: Listen-Tests, Curriculum, and Results for the Thinking Improvement Project." In *Highlights of the 1968 IRA Preconvention Institute II: Critical Reading and Listening,* pp. 43-70. Salt Lake City: Exemplary Center for Reading, 1969. (b)
Lists objectives in tentative sequence for a general listening program and a critical listening program. Describes tests and reports experimental results.

Lundsteen, S. W. *Basic Annotated Bibliography on Listening.* Urbana, Ill.: NCTE and ERIC, 1969. (c)

Lundsteen, S. W. "Manipulating Abstract Thinking as a Subability to Problem Solving in a Problem Solving Context of an English Curriculum." *American Educational Research Journal* 7 (May 1970): 373-96. (a)
Describes the major analysis in the Thinking Improvement Project, one portion of which was devoted to promoting listening skills as a subability to creative problem solving.

Lundsteen, S. W. "Promoting Growth in Problem Solving in an Integrated Program of Language Skills for Fifth Grade." Paper presented at the Annual Meeting of the International Reading Association, Anaheim, California, May 1970. [ED 045 301] (b)

Lundsteen, S. W. *Children Learn to Communicate.* Englewood Cliffs, N.J.: Prentice-Hall, 1976. (a)
  An elementary language arts textbook for teacher training. The central focus of the book is an approach to the language arts through creative problem solving for which listening is one subskill.

Lundsteen, S. W. *Ideas Into Practice.* Englewood Cliffs, N.J.: Prentice-Hall, 1976. (b)
  Contains a unit of listening lessons (pp. 137-218), including the making of a unit and a tentative hierarchy of listening subskills. Lessons deal with differences between listening and hearing; use of leftover thinking space; group interactive listening and consensus; two-way responsibility while listening for details, sequences, and main ideas; self-evaluation of listening skills; inference making while listening, assumption making, and many enrichment activities that interrelate listening with the other language arts and children's literature.

Lundsteen, S. W. "On Developmental Relations between Language Learning and Reading." *The Elementary School Journal* 77 (1977): 192-203.

Lundsteen, S. W., and N. Bernstein-Tarrow. *Guiding Young Children's Learning.* New York: McGraw-Hill, in press.

Markle, S. M. "Some Thoughts on Task Analysis and Objectives in Educational Psychology." *Educational Psychologist* 10 (1973): 24-29.

Markle, S. M., and P. W. Tieman. *Instructor Manual: Really Understanding Concepts.* 2d ed. Champaign, Ill.: Stipes Publishing Company, 1970.
  Gives examples of concept analysis, interpretation of errors, and criterion exercises for constructing an instructional analysis of a concept. Also see their paper "Some Principles of Instructional Design at Higher Cognitive Levels," for the International Congress for Instructional Technology, Berlin, 1972, which contains a concept analysis of "morpheme."

Marks, E., and G. A. Noll. "Procedures and Criteria for Evaluating Reading and Listening Comprehension Tests." *Educational and Psychological Measurement* 27 (Summer 1967): 335-48.

Masur, E. F. "Preschool Boys' Speech Modifications: The Effect of Listeners' Linguistic Levels and Conversational Responsiveness." *Child Development* 49 (September 1978): 924-27.

McCullough, C. M. *Preparation of Textbooks in the Mother Tongue.* Newark, Del.: International Reading Association, 1968. [ED 011 826]
  See "Thought Patterns in Expository Writing" (pp. 98-114), which also can be applied to spoken discourse.

McKee, N. "Susan, Touch Your Toes." *Texas Outlook* 52 (May 1967): 58.
  Describes use of principal's intercom loudspeaker for listening practice.

162   *References*

Mead, N. A. "Issues Related to Assessing Listening Ability." Paper presented at the Annual Meeting of the American Educational Research Association, Toronto, Canada, April 1978.

Monaghan, R. R., and J. G. Martin. "Symbolic Interaction: Analysis of Listening." *Journal of Communication* 18 (June 1968): 127-30.
Poses two main questions: What is an effective listener? and What are the distinguishing characteristics of persons who are effective listeners and those who are not? Draws up a working list of topics and some references which might provide an outline for study at the college level. Sample research strategies generated: repertory grid projective devices, inferences of hypnagogically-induced images.

Morris, C., and R. Harrison. "Information as a Construct in the Study of Communication." Paper presented at a meeting of the National Society for the Study of Communication, New York, April 1968.
Presents ways "information" has been used as a construct and suggests new avenues of research in human communication, especially tapping the internal storehouse of knowledge and prior learning through projective techniques.

National Assessment of Educational Progress. "Pilot Study Explores Speaking, Listening Skills." *National Assessment Newsletter* 11 (1978): 4.

Neisser, U. *Cognitive Psychology.* New York: Appleton-Century-Crofts, 1967.

Neville, M. H., and A. K. Puch. "Context in Reading and Listening: A Comparison of Children's Errors in Cloze Tests." *British Journal of Educational Psychology* 44 (November 1974): 224-32.

Norton, D., and W. R. Hodgson. "Intelligibility of Black and White Speakers for Black and White Listeners." *Language and Speech* 16 (July-September 1974): 207-10.

Oakland, T. "Relationships between Social Class and Phonemic and Nonphonemic Auditory Discrimination Ability." Paper presented to a meeting of the American Educational Research Association, Los Angeles, February 1969. [ED 031 383]

Olsen, J. "How to Help Your Pupils Pay Attention." *Grade Teacher* 84 (September 1966): 148+.
Suggests that listening requires training and is not governed by IQ. Teachers can build listening activities into regular work by remembering that interesting topics make interested listeners and that they should use materials, articles, stories, and essays related to any field pupils are studying. Gives suggested activities.

Olsen, M. R. "A Program of Instructional Activities for the Development of Listening Skills in Preschool Children." Ph.D. dissertation, University of Utah, 1973.

Orange County Office of the Superintendent of Schools. *Children and Listening Centers: Why, How, What.* Orange County, Calif.: Orange County Schools, 1966.
> Examines ways children may use listening centers more creatively.

Orr, D. B., and W. R. Graham. "Development of a Listening Comprehension Test to Identify Educational Potential among Disadvantaged Junior High School Students." *American Educational Research Journal* 5 (March 1968): 167-80.
> Describes the development of a listening comprehension test based upon the hypothesis that for disadvantaged children a listening test with appropriate content would be more suitable than the usual aptitude or achievement tests as a measure of their academic potential.

Ostermeier, T. H. "An Experimental Study on the Type and Frequency of Reference as Used by an Unfamiliar Source in a Message Effect upon Perceived Credibility and Attitude Change." Ph.D. dissertation, Michigan State University, 1966. Also in *Speech Monographs* 34 (1967): 257.

Pflaumer, E. M. "A Definition of Listening." Master's thesis, Ohio State University, 1968.
> Describes and includes a Q-Sort, a measure by which an individual can create a visual model of his or her attitude about topics and situations as he or she describes it by sorting statements into piles. The author related Marshall McLuhan's concepts of "implosion" and "self-amptation" to findings. A unique addition to the literature.

Piaget, J. *Science of Education and the Psychology of the Child.* New York: Orion Press, 1970.

Ratcliff, J. D. "I Am Joe's Ear." *Reader's Digest,* October 1971, pp. 131-34.

Reuter, A. "Listening Experiences: Instructional Materials Center Dial-A-Tape System Advances Learning." *Elementary English* 46 (November 1969): 905-6.

Robeck, M. C., and J. A. R. Wilson. *Psychology of Reading: Foundations for Instruction.* New York: Wiley, 1974.
> Chapter six contains a discussion of auditory perception including a suggested sequence for learning decoding, discrimination, association of sound and letter, the latter a discovery technique of teaching association so that the child is made ready for conceptualizations of the structure of word parts. This technique includes self-discovery of the sound-letter relations in order to promote transfer to new situations.

Robinson, H. A., and A. T. Burrows. *Teacher Effectiveness in Elementary Language Arts: A Progress Report.* Urbana, Ill.: National Conference on Research in English and ERIC/RCS, 1974.

Rosner, J. *The Development and Validation of an Individualized Perceptual Skills Curriculum.* Pittsburgh, Pa.: University of Pittsburgh Learning Research and Development Center, 1972. Also see the Research and Development Center report by J. Rosner and D. P. Simon, *The Auditory Analysis Test: An Initial Report,* 1971.

Rosnow, R. "Poultry and Prejudice." *Psychology Today,* vol. 5, no. 10 (1972): 53-56.

Ross, M., and G. G. Thomas. *Auditory Management of Hearing-Impaired Children: Principles and Prerequisites for Intervention.* Baltimore, Md.: University Park Press, 1978.

Rossiter, C. M., Jr. "Chronological Age and Listening of Adult Students." *Adult Education* 21 (Fall 1970): 40-43.
Listening ability apparently declines with age: older students may be retaining less from oral presentations of information than younger students.

Roswell, F. G., and G. Natchez. *Reading Disability: A Human Approach to Learning.* 3d ed. New York: Basic Books, 1977.

Ruddell, R. B. "Oral Language and the Development of Other Language Skills." *Elementary English* 43 (May 1966): 489-98.
Reviews a number of studies on the relationship between listening and reading, as well as other linguistic relations.

Russell, D. H. "A Conspectus of Recent Research on Listening Abilities." *Elementary English* 41 (March 1964): 262-67.
A comprehensive and carefully wrought review.

Russell, D. H., and H. R. Fea. "Research on Teaching Reading." In *Handbook of Research on Teaching,* edited by N. L. Gage. Chicago: Rand McNally, 1963.
See section on auditory perception.

Russell, D. H., and E. F. Russell. *Listening Aids through the Grades.* New York: Bureau of Publications, Teachers College, Columbia University, 1959.
Contains the most complete and comprehensive collection of listening activities in existence. Divided into primary and intermediate grades and into levels of listening skill. Informative introduction includes an analysis of similarities and differences between reading and listening. Over one hundred activities listed.

Samuels, S. J. "Factors Which Influence the Word Recognition Process of Skilled Readers." Paper presented at National Reading Conference, Atlanta, December 4, 1969.
Contains sections on active process, context, a three-stage model for recognition (information use, hypothesis, test procedure), meaningful material—all of which are also relevant to the listening process.

Sanders, D. A. *Auditory Perception of Speech: An Introduction to Principles and Problems.* Englewood Cliffs, N.J.: Prentice-Hall, 1977.
> Concerned with the nature of speech perception, auditory learning, and associated problems. Focus is on the neurophysiological, psycho-acoustic, and psycholinguistic aspects of the auditory processing of speech. Describes current research knowledge and indicates directions of future research and methodology.

Sarbin, T. R. "Role Theory." In *Handbook of Social Psychology,* vol. 1, edited by G. Lindzey, pp. 223-58. Cambridge, Mass.: Addison-Wesley, 1954.

Schlawin, S., C. Chew, and J. C. Crabtree. *Listening and Speaking, K-3: A Packet for Teachers.* Albany, N. Y.: State University of New York and the State Education Department, Bureau of Elementary Curriculum Development, 1975.

Schmidt, B. "The Relationship between Questioning Levels, Strategies, and Listening Comprehension in K-3 Children." Ph.D. dissertation, University of California, Berkeley, 1972.
> Children ages five to nine were trained by their teachers for eight weeks in factual, interpretive, and applicative listening comprehension. Teachers were trained in using a matrix of levels of questioning strategies related to the research of Taba (see reference). Verifying the earlier Taba research, those teachers who extended and tried to lift the level of questioning did obtain higher abstract levels as shown in pupil responses, rather than merely the lower, concrete levels of thought. Those teachers who used controlling behaviors and asked rhetorical questions stifled children's responses (e.g., "That was a good story, wasn't it, boys and girls?"). Results from observing and rating the video tapes of teachers, however, did not reveal any statistical differences among them. However, some marked differences appeared among their pupils. An examination of pupil variables of sex and socioeconomic status suggested that these variables apparently had no effect on the pupils' performance. However, the variable of age (as might be expected) was significantly related to performance on the test of factual, interpretive, and applicative listening comprehension. (Also see the final USOE report from the University of California, *Berkeley Project Delta, Developing Excellence in Literacy Teaching Abilities,* 1970, directed by R. B. Ruddell; this dissertation was a part of the USOE study.)

Schneeberg, H. "Listening While Reading: A Four Year Study." *The Reading Teacher* 30 (March 1977): 629-35.

Science Research Associates. *The Listening Skills Program.* Palo Alto, Calif.: Science Research Associates, 1969.
> Presents a multi-level and multi-skill program for each grade level, one through nine. Skills include auditory discrimination, story sequence, main idea, cause and effect, creative listening, and critical listening on tape, record, or cassette. Includes teacher manual for each level.

Seymour, D. "What Do You Mean, 'Auditory Perception'?" *Elementary School Journal* 70 (1970): 175-79.

Short, S. "Audio Speedteach." *Media and Methods* 9 (March 1973): 63, 65-66, 68.

Siebert, W. F. *Instructional Television: The Best of ERIC.* Lafayette, Ind.: Purdue University, Measurement and Research Center, April 1972.
    This publication represented a collection of the best ERIC documents concerning instructional television.

Silverstone, D. M. "Compressed Speech: Capabilities and Uses." *Audiovisual Instruction* 19 (January 1974): 42-43.
    Suggests that compressed speech encourages development of powers of concentration.

Smith, F. "Making Sense of Reading—And of Reading Instruction." *Harvard Educational Review* 47 (1977): 386-95.

Smith, T. W. "Auding and Reading Skills as Sources of Cultural Bias in the Davis-Eells Games and California Test of Mental Maturity." Ph.D. dissertation, University of Southern California, 1956. (Excerpted in *Listening Readings,* edited by S. Duker, 1966.)
    Listening skill (as well as reading skill) revealed significant source of intelligence test bias when the Gates Silent Reading Test and the memory section of California Mental Maturity Test were administered orally at varying cultural levels.

Solly, C. M., and C. M. Murphy. *The Development of the Perceptual World.* New York: Basic Books, 1960.

Spearritt, D. "A Factorial Analysis of Listening Comprehension." Ph.D. dissertation, Harvard University, 1961. Also: *Listening Comprehension—A Factorial Analysis.* ACER Research Series No. 76. Melbourne, Australia: Australian Council for Educational Research, 1962.
    A factor analysis, apparently yielding a "listening comprehension" factor, employed correlations from 34 tests given to 300 sixth grade pupils.

Stammer, John D. "Target: The Basics of Listening." *Language Arts* 54 (September 1977): 661-64.

Stanners, R. F., and others. "The Pupillary Response to Sentences: Influences of Listening Set and Deep Structure." *Journal of Verbal Learning and Verbal Behavior* 11 (April 1972): 257-68.

Stark, J. "An Investigation of the Relationship of the Vocal and Communicative Aspects of Speech Competency with Listening Comprehension." *Speech Monographs* 24 (June 1957): 98-99.

Stern, C. "Children's Auditory Discrimination Inventory (CADI)." Mimeographed. University of California, Los Angeles, June 1969.

Describes the problems in constructing an auditory discrimination inventory, especially regarding deprived children, and the development of a new one.

Stewig, J. W. "Language Growth through Creative Dramatics." Paper presented at the NCTE National Conference on the Language Arts in the Elementary School, St. Louis, Missouri, March 7, 1970.

Discusses creative improvisation and interpretation, an exemplary program, vocabulary growth, paralanguage, kinesics, and spontaneous oral composition and gives many references.

Sticht, T. G. "Learning by Listening in Relation to Aptitude, Reading and Rate-Controlled Speech." Technical Report 69-23, HumRRO Division No. 3, December 1969. [ED 037 666]

Found that moderate degrees of speech compression (275 wpm) may improve listening efficiency (amount learned per minute of listening) for men of high, average, and low aptitudes unless material is of very low redundancy. Also see Professional Paper 4-70, "Studies on the Efficiency of Learning by Listening to Time-Compressed Speech," February 1970; and Technical Report 71-5, "Learning by Listening in Relation to Aptitude, Reading, and Rate-Controlled Speech: Additional Studies," April 1971.

Sticht, T. G., L. Beck, R. H. Hauke, G. M. Kleiman, and J. H. James. *Auding and Reading: A Developmental Model.* Arlington, Va.: Human Resource Research Organization, 1974.

Stiggins, J., L. K. Allal, M. J. Gordon, and J. L. Byers. "Effectiveness of Verbal Communication among Elementary School Pupils, Teachers and Teacher Aides." Paper presented to the American Educational Research Association, New York, 1971.

Describes a study among first and third grade black pupils at an inner city school which had instituted mixed-age "family" grouping at the start of the school year. Teacher aides comprehended pupil speech as effectively as teachers. Older pupils did not appear to be able to replace adults as the most effective source of information for completion of a picture designation task, but the older pupils offered better instructional assistance than the first grade listeners' peers.

Strickland, R. G. "The Language of Elementary School Children: Its Relationship to the Language of Reading Textbooks and the Quality of Reading of Selected Children." *Viewpoints: Bulletin of the School of Education, Indiana University* 38 (1962): pp. 85-86. [ED 002 970]

Taba, H. "Teaching Strategies and Cognitive Functioning in Elementary School Children." USOE Cooperative Research Project No. 2404, San Francisco State College, 1966.

   In a normal classroom setting the researcher appraised certain ideas about the development of thinking and examined the effects of planned teaching strategies on the development of children's thought. She presents modifications on her earlier major tool of a coding system for classroom transactions and describes teacher-training materials designed to lead students to master the abstract and symbolic form of thought much earlier and more systematically than could be expected if this development were left solely to the accidents of experience or to less appropriate strategies. Both control and experimental groups were used in this study.

Tapp, J. L. "Children Can Understand Rumor." *Social Education* 17 (April 1953): 163-64.

   A description of a lesson.

Taylor, C. W. "Listening Creatively." *Instructor* 73 (February 1964): 5, 103-4.

   Suggests that a person's mind set can affect the creativeness of reception. Listening to learn and master information differs from listening to stimulate one's own creative thinking and imagination. Gives suggested activities.

Taylor, C. W., W. R. Smith, B. Ghiselin, B. V. Sheets, and J. R. Cochran. *Identification of Communication Abilities in Military Situations.* USAF WADC Technical Report No. 58-92, 1958.

Taylor, K. K. "Auding and Reading." *Research in the Teaching of English* 10 (1976): 75-78.

Taylor, S. E. *Listening: What Research Says to the Teacher, #29.* Washington, D.C.: National Education Association, 1964. [ED 026 120]

   Indicates how research findings may help with the problems of the classroom teacher. Covers factors which may influence hearing, listening, and auding. Suggests a program to improve listening. The section in this book on operational definition draws upon information in this pamphlet.

Thames, K. H., and C. M. Rossiter. "The Effects of Reading Practice with Compressed Speech on Reading Rate and Listening Comprehension." *AV Communication Review* 20 (Spring 1972): 35-42.

   Concluded that reading practice with accompanying compressed speech as a pacer resulted in a significant increase in reading rate without loss in comprehension for the experimental group when compared with the control group. Delayed post-test indicated that this gain was not temporary. This study bears replicating.

Thayer, L. "Theory-Building in Communication: IV—Some Observations and Speculations." Paper presented at the Sixteenth Annual Conference of the National Society for the Study of Communication, New York, April 1968.

Trebilcock, E. L. "Can Auding by Kindergarten Children Be Improved in a Normal Classroom Situation through Direct Teaching of This Skill?" *Dissertation Abstracts* 31 (1970): 687A.

Tyler, L. L., and F. M. Klein. *Recommendations for Curriculum and Instructional Materials.* Los Angeles: Tyler Press, 1971.
    Guidelines for evaluating curriculum materials. The recommendations specify approved ideas in seven categories: general, specifications, rationale, appropriateness, effectiveness, conditions, and practicality. Recommendations within each category are designated essential, very desirable, and desirable.

Vygotsky, L. *Thought and Language.* Cambridge, Mass.: MIT Press, 1962.

Waller, T. G. *Think First, Read Later! Piagetian Prerequisites for Reading.* Newark, Del.: International Reading Association, 1977.

Wallner, N. K. "The Development of a Listening Comprehension Test for Kindergarten and Beginning First Grade." *Educational and Psychological Measurement* 34 (Summer 1974): 391-6.

Walsh, G. "Leader Must Respond to Feeling and Content." *College University Business* 49 (October 1970): 62-64.

Weaver, S. W., and W. L. Rutherford. "A Hierarchy of Listening Skills." *Elementary English* 51 (November-December 1974): 1146-50.
    An important and needed compendium, categorized as to environmental skills, discrimination skills, and comprehension skills, from prenatal to grades four through six.

Wetstone, H. S., and B. Z. Friedlander. "The Effects of Live, TV, and Audio Story Narration on Primary Grade Children's Listening Comprehension." *Journal of Education Research* 68 (1974): 32-35.

Wilkinson, A. "Listening and the Discriminative Response." *California English Journal* 5 (December 1969): 7-20.
    Discusses various registers and situations in discourse, the difference between spoken and written language, the implications for testing, the teaching of oracy (as a counterpart to literacy), and gives samples from interesting tests developed in England.

Wilt, M. E. "Teach Listening?" *Grade Teacher* 81 (April 1964): 51, 93-94.
    Suggests ways to prevent deterioration in listening skills which occurs as children learn to read and write. Lists of activities and means of informal measurement are presented by one of the pioneers in the field.

Witkin, B. R. "Auditory Perception—Implications for Language Development." *Journal of Research and Development in Education* 3 (Fall 1969): 53-68.
    Presents research, describes new tests and materials, and gives implications for education in the areas of (1) attention to competing messages, (2) compressed speech or increase in rate of material, (3) auditory discrimination, and (4) auditory sequencing. Many of the significant

references in these areas are mentioned in this article and were excluded
from the present bibliography. Other articles in the Fall issue also deal
with listening.

Witkin, B. R. *Reading Improvement through Auditory Perceptual Training.*
USOE Title III Project No. 0471. Hayward, Calif.: Alameda County
School Department, 1972.